Reviews for
Be Outrageous: Do the Impossible

Jean gently builds the case for listening to our inner voice and gives us building blocks of questions and examinations to break down the thoughts and perceptions that create internal blocks. She provides real life examples that help us see and feel and touch what we deeply, soulfully seek. I highly recommend this work: delightful, fun, and life changing.

—Patricia Gilbers, Author *The Isabella Willow Romantic Suspense* series

This book teaches the reader to believe in himself and follow his passion. After reading this book the idea of living a mundane life seems outrageous. Jean's point that we are all made for greatness and her encouragement to follow our inner vision is powerful. In it she gives the reader exercises to bring that vision to life. This is a must read for people who want to blast through self-doubt. I loved it!

—John Gillardi, Executive Leader, Big 4 Accounting Firm

In Jean Walters' book Be Outrageous: Do the Impossible, *she makes spiritual teaching understandable to every reader. Being a gifted teacher and counselor, Jean shares the culmination of her experience in mentoring people in their quest to live authentically and follow their dreams. This has been Jean's passion and life work and now she shares this knowledge with anyone fortunate enough to read her book. Through examples and inspiration, Jean shows us that doing the seemingly impossible is not beyond our abilities. It is as simple as following your dream!*

—Jo Wolken, Sales Account Executive and Truth Seeker

This book encourages the reader to put aside his uncertainty, small thinking, and fear and take on a greater vision. Every person who wants to rid himself of self-defeating beliefs must read this book. Truly inspirational!
—Diane Carson, President PromoXpertz LLC

Jean brings home the truth that whatever we can conceive and believe, we can achieve. The stories contained in this book will fill your soul and inspire you to realize your own kind of greatness. It helped me clarify my goals and it will help you too.
—Becky Noelker, Becky Noelker Interior Design

Jean reaches into the corners of your mind and finds the puzzle pieces that need to come together for you to live a life of passion and fulfillment. You can't read this book without wanting to be more. The stories within its covers will touch your heart and open your mind to possibilities.
—Reverend Pat Powers, Spiritual Director,
Radiance Center for Spiritual Living

I love the theme that is carried throughout this book. You are a magnificent being capable of achieving any goal you choose to pursue. I felt empowered as I read these words. Thank you for this book.
—Karen S Hoffman, Founder Gateway to Dreams

Inspire, motivate and educate! Be Outrageous: Do the Impossible *does it all. It instructs you on how to trust your dream. That is powerful!*
—Sonja Shin, Mental Health Advocate and Spiritual Coach

BE
OUTRAGEOUS:
DO THE IMPOSSIBLE

*. . . others have and
you can too!*

Jean Walters

Be Outrageous: Do the Impossible
...others have and you can too!
Jean Walters
Inner Connections

Published by Inner Connections, St. Louis, MO

Editor: Anne Cote, ac1313@juno.com
Cover and interior design: Davis Creative, DavisCreative.com

Library of Congress Cataloging-in-Publication Data
Library of Congress Control Number: 2016914211
Jean Walters
Be Outrageous: Do the Impossible ...others have and you can too!
ISBN: 978-0-9979375-4-1
Library of Congress subject headings:
     1. SEL021000 2. SEL000000 3. OCC019000

2016

ATTENTION CORPORATIONS, UNIVERSITIES, COLLEGES AND PROFESSIONAL ORGANIZATIONS: Quantity discounts are available on bulk purchases of this book for educational, gift purposes, or as premiums for increasing magazine subscriptions or renewals. Special books or book excerpts can also be created to fit specific needs. For information, please contact Inner Connections, jean@spiritualtransformation.com

Dedication

*I dedicate this book to all
the outrageous people in the world
who have had a dream
and followed it no matter what.
You are our teachers.*

Table of Contents

Sharon –

Be your outrageous
self!

Love,
Jen Wattler
2019

Acknowledgments

Thank you to all the people who have told me their stories and allowed me to share these in my writings. Your generosity has been a light to others.

I have been privileged to know many outrageous people. These are the ones who set a goal and move toward it no matter what mountain they had to climb to get there. It has been fun to be in a "helping" role as you create your impossible dream. I love your determination, your brilliance and your light. You are my inspiration.

As you can see, I have been the beneficiary of an amazing career in assisting others discover and implement their dreams. What an honor. Thanks to every client and student who has shown up and permitted me to share in their journey of discovery. Your efforts have been empowering.

I acknowledge the enthusiastic and tenacious efforts of my editor, Anne Cote. She is an amazing teacher and a great friend. I am grateful for the support and wisdom of Cathy Davis and her team at Davis Creative for designing an incredible, step-by-step process for getting this and many other books out to the world. Cathy has the great gift of making things seem easier than they appear to be. We need a lot more of that in the world.

And most of all thank you to all the people who have encouraged me and believed in my message. I am so delighted you are in my world.

*Inherently, each one of us has the substance within
to achieve whatever our goals and dreams define.
What is missing from each of us is the training,
education, knowledge and insight
to utilize what we already have.*

—Mark Twain, Author and Humorist

*The potential of the average person is like
a huge ocean unsoiled, a new continent unexplored,
a world of possibility waiting to be released and
channeled toward some great good.*

—Brian Tracy, Author

■

Introduction

You, Too, Can Do The Impossible
Discover and Achieve Your Dream

When I was a young girl, I went to the public library every week. I loved to read. I was very specific in my choice of reading material: always biographies or autobiographies of successful and/or famous people. I was searching for something. How did they know what to do? How did they accomplish their great feats? I was fascinated with the idea that an ordinary farmer, printer, housewife, or even child, could make dramatic differences in their culture, nation, or world. It still fascinates me.

What I have discovered along the way is that each person has a calling in his soul, something that he is designed to do and something that speaks to him specifically. In all the thousands, perhaps millions, of people I have had contact with in my years of counseling and coaching, instructing businesses, and teaching the masses, I have learned this: There are no ordinary people. Everyone has greatness within. Every person can choose to follow that call or let fear or self-doubt block the way. It is an individual decision. Yet, when one is called to do something or play a role, that person does not rest well until they respond to that impulse.

When I researched success as a child, I found Abigail Adams, wife of President John Adams, exceedingly resourceful and inspiring. She worked with what she had and hung her laundry on ropes rigged in the Oval Office. Can you imagine anyone getting by with that today? Resourcefulness—using what is available—has always been one of my favorite qualities. Being outrageous is another. I follow with some outrageous stories of people who accomplished the seemingly impossible.

Doing the impossible means different things to different people. Someone might think being a millionaire is impossible, and thus a great accomplishment. Another individual may want to bring clean water to an African village or supply books to children who have none.

Mohandas Gandhi was painfully shy. The idea of standing before people seemed impossible. Yet, he had a passion that required it. His desire to share his idea of non-violent resistance to British rule, which dominated India, drove him in front of audiences again and again. This calling brought this shy, humble man out of obscurity to being credited with his country's ultimate freedom over British rule.

Mother Teresa brought a loving heart to the indigent in India and won the attention of the world. Her mission and vision was to aid the poor and sick. In the process, she helped thousands, perhaps millions of people through the charities she established in numerous countries.

Others, like Sam Walton, possessed a drive to bring reasonably priced merchandise to rural communities. He started with a store in Bentonville, Arkansas, his hometown. From there, Wal-Mart became a national leader in merchandising, and Walton became a billionaire.

Joy Mangano is a more current example of setting a vision and accomplishing it, despite blocks and obstacles along the way. Mangano is an inventor. She did not have training to be an inventor, nor was she trained to be an engineer, for that matter. What she had was inventiveness, relentlessness, and determination. In her role as a housewife, she was creatively inspired to develop laborsaving devices. The first one was the Miracle Mop. She *knew* that housewives would want it for its clean design and sophistication. She pushed forward relentlessly until she was on national television, selling her mop to a major audience. She has since developed numerous other laborsaving devices and products while becoming a millionaire many times over. Presently, there is a movie outlining her story. It is called *JOY*, which happens to be an apt description of this powerhouse.

Dealing with naysayers is a small part of the process. The most intelligent, creative people in history have had naysayers. A legendary example is inventor Thomas Edison. His teachers said that he was too stupid to learn anything. He did not agree. His conclusion was, "I never failed." He knew that each experiment he conducted led to the next and the next, and it would all end in the discovery he sought. In his mind, there were no failures. He needed each step to reach his ultimate success.

Someone pointed out to Edison that he had failed ten thousand times in developing the storage battery. Edison responded that he hadn't failed. "I just found ten thousand ways that won't work." His belief was that he "failed his way to success." Even the disadvantage of deafness, which would have stopped many others, did not seem to faze him. By the world's standards, he was capable of little. Yet, he found his own methods of self-education and innovation, using them to patent over 1,093 inventions.

Abraham Lincoln was also brilliant and ambitious, even though he possessed little formal education. His determination led him to read by the light of a candle so that he could self-educate. In many people's estimation, he was a failure because he was unsuccessful in business several times, had a nervous breakdown at twenty-seven, and lost eight times in his attempts to win a government office. Yet, Lincoln did not let these losses deter him. He followed his conscience and values and has since been deemed one of the greatest presidents to serve his country. I am quite sure he would say that all of those attempts were necessary to build his mental muscles and create the power of leadership he demonstrated.

Walt Disney, the founder of Disneyland, Disney World, and a massive motion-picture industry, also failed many times before he made it big. In his formative years, he was fired from a newspaper job because he lacked imagination. Fortunately, Disney did not accept that pronouncement. He was not even discouraged when he went bankrupt several times. He had a vision and was determined to bring it to form. He stated, "It is kind of fun to do the impossible."

Then, there was Babe Ruth, the homerun king *and* the strikeout king as well. Does anyone remember the strikeouts?

Of course, no one can deny that a poor black girl raised in Mississippi by her single mother and her grandmother, a maid, achieved the seemingly impossible when she was given her own television talk show. Later, Oprah Winfrey developed a cable network and became the first black female billionaire.

There are inspiring people in every avenue of life, people who followed their inner voice and accomplished amazing things.

This book is about these kinds of outrageous individuals who set out to follow their dreams and then ended up doing the impossible. Perhaps you can catch glimpses of their thinking and drive. Perhaps you will identify with some of them and be reminded of your outrageous dream and decide to go for it.

The idea is that you have the same stuff that they do. With their stories and the principles outlined in this book, I hope to inspire you to discover your calling and pay attention to your fantasies, knowing that they are in your mind as a gift from the Universe. Through this recognition, you will be able to give birth to the glorious life you were meant to live. Perhaps, in that way, you can do what might seem impossible today. That is my hope for you.

Every person has a unique idea of what the impossible looks like. One person wants to help sick children, and another, like Bill Gates, wanted to put a computer in every home. We march to different drummers. As we listen to our hearts, we discover our impossible dream. This I know for sure: whatever you dream, you can achieve because you are never given a dream without having the ability to fulfill it. Never!

This book is to give you the keys to uncovering your seemingly impossible dream and to manifest it. I wish you great success in your journey.

*When I examine myself and my methods of thought,
I come to the conclusion that the gift of fantasy
has meant more to me than my talent for absorbing
positive knowledge.*

Albert Einstein, Theoretical Physicist

*When one links job satisfaction to financial
compensation, they are never paid enough. Yet, when
they see work as a way to dance with life, meet new
people, and unleash the creative tiger within,
they become very rich indeed.*

Mike Dooley, *Notes from the Universe*

■

Chapter One

What Is Your Impossible Dream?

We discover that doing the impossible is a relative term. For one person, achieving a college education may seem outrageous, given the circumstances, while for FedEx Founder Frederick W. Smith, establishing a worldwide delivery service was his impossible dream.

The important thing is to not second-guess your dream, because with the accomplishment of one goal, you will have grown the muscles and drive to move to the next. The main thing is to accept that there is no randomness in what you seek. Your desire comes from your soul and it is valid and achievable. It was doable for the people mentioned in this book and it is attainable for you as well.

Crossing boundaries, going for your dream, and saying "No" to limitation, that is the key. We all have it in us. We can do the things we have fantasized because dreams are not random. They are specialized and individualized.

My dream was to change the world by empowering people and bringing them hope. I have done that through counseling, coaching, teaching, psychic readings, and writing for over thirty-five years. Someone else's aspiration, such as Arnold Schwarzenegger's, to be exact, was to be a movie star and millionaire. Another person, author-teacher Mike Dooley, wanted to travel the world. Both accomplished their goals. The point is that *your* dreams and ambitions are specifically designed for *you*, and you would not have them without possessing everything you need to accomplish them.

It could be that being outrageous is simply breaking societal rules. I have heard the story numerous times about the six- or seven-year-old child who is instructed to confess his sins. (I ask you, what sin can a child this young commit?) Yet, it is an assignment. These children are to peruse their minds and come up with a sin, and if that isn't bad enough, they have to confess it out loud to a big, powerful adult authority figure. It is scary because having a sin and confessing it is a required activity. The children don't want to come up short and blow the assignment.

To fail this task is to endure disapproval from a high church official. Many pass the test by lying, by making up sins. It is all they've got, and you have to admit it is a creative way to get through it.

The bottom line is that the child is taught to focus on what they have done wrong. The indication is that they better admit something and come clean or they are in big trouble.

This mental exercise has created many guilt-ridden, anxious people because, as children, we place great faith in the adults who instruct us. It may take years or possibly never for individuals to break free of the fear that they are sinful beings. In the meantime, while they worry about that, they are not focusing on their creative talents and brilliance. This crazy exercise is just one example of how a person can lose track of what they came into this world to experience. Of course, there are many others.

This chapter is about discerning your dreams and eliminating anything that has gotten in the way of their fulfillment. By doing this work, you will regain the momentum to recommit, take control, and move forward in your quest. Your job is to unravel the confusion and to adjust your life projectory, so that you unquestionably trust yourself and all that has been given you in order to live the amazing life for which you have been designed. If you have to dump a negative program along the way, so much the better. So let's get on with it.

There are many wonderful stories in this book to help you identify your desire. Perhaps you will relate to some of the people or connect with their journey. Perhaps you will remember what it is that you have always felt and wanted. Or possibly, you will be inspired to come up with a new idea.

It is important to remember that your dream is the right one for you. It has emerged from deep within you. Dreams are selective and specialized, perfectly formulated to work with your exact talents and abilities. You were designed for them and they for you.

Academy Award movie director Spike Lee said, "I didn't find film. Film found me."

That is how it works. The idea is to lower your resistance and let your dream find you. Generally, that means letting go of fear, old irrelevant mental programs, and limiting tribal beliefs, so that you can brazenly take steps to move in the direction of your dream.

An old saying is: *For every step you take, God takes two.* In other words, the Universe supports you and helps you find your way. The common element in every achiever is focus. They focus on what they want and they walk toward it. Sometimes they fall down along the way. But they always get up more times than they fall down, and through persistent effort, they reach their goals.

I had a client, Helene, who had diligently studied for her real-estate exam. She wanted to get her license so she could sell real estate and support her family. She knew the material and understood real-estate law, but she froze when taking the test for her license and, consequently, failed to pass. By the time she came to me, she had failed the exam several times. You might say she had *test-anxiety* since she routinely forgot everything when under the gun to complete the test. I ultimately made an autosuggestion audio tape which Helene listened to diligently. It helped her relax, see herself answering the questions correctly, and excitedly receiving her license.

Once Helene replaced her old program of fear and incapacitation with a new positive one that registered her ability, and then accepted her vision of selling real estate, she was on her way. That is when she made her breakthrough. Her mental program of *I-don't-believe-I-can-do-this* was replaced with a new one that projected her successful completion: a new program and a new vision. A new life.

We all have ideas and limitations regarding who we are and what we can or cannot do. These concepts have come from everywhere: our families, teachers, friends, random people on the street, movies, television, even religion—everywhere. We can respond to life as robots following these erroneous scripts, or we can challenge them and ask why. "Why can't I climb to the top of the mountain or to the top of my industry? Why can't I invent something that will change the world? Why can't I negotiate a peace agreement between nations? Why can't I have a successful career as a real estate agent?"

You get it! It is about challenging the status quo and all the negative beliefs that have been planted in a vulnerable young mind, and about being willing to strike out in a new direction.

Remember, when someone tells you it won't work and you can't do it, they are really speaking about themselves. To be specific, it won't work for them and it can't happen to them. That is the belief they nurture. It does not have to be yours.

I had another client, Patrice, who owned her own real-estate company. She ignored all the negative suggestions that came from people. When she would hear, "Money is tight. You won't be able to get a loan," she would remember that the person speaking was just informing her of what that person believed. In Patrice's experience, she would weekly receive phone calls from lenders offering to provide money. Patrice became a very successful real-estate broker-owner of many properties because she believed in her dream and she kept walking toward it.

If you want to learn to swim, you start by jumping in the shallow water and kicking your feet. You might add floating on your back or kicking across the pool on a flotation device. One step at a time. Or you can jump in the deep water and frantically flail until you reach shore. Which method speaks to you? We often use both.

The point is, you choose your goal and you can make it hard. You go it alone or simplify the steps and even reach out for help. Assistance is always available. It definitely shortens the distance from where you are to where you want to be. The nature of the Universe is such that, once you have declared your desire, help is provided. If you are not too proud to admit that you could use some assistance, people often come out of the woodwork with gems of wisdom, a helping hand, a referral, the right mentor, school, book, class, or workshop that is just right.

I once had a student who was a single mother with three children. She was adamant that she wanted to return to school to earn her master's degree but did not have money to pay for the education. My suggestion was that she check into the possibility of getting a scholarship or grant money that was set up for single moms to return to school. I thought surely educational institutions would offer an opportunity applicable to her situation. She followed up with the local university and, sure enough, she received a full scholarship for her masters' program. Sometimes, it is as simple as stating a desire and someone will have a resource or idea that never occurred to the person looking for a solution. It happens all the time.

Anything is possible. Whatever you want to achieve, think of every possibility for getting it. Take the first step, then the next.

What is it you want to achieve? What does it look like and feel like? Visualize the exact outcome and soon an idea, a resource, or a person will show up to lend a helping hand. Try it—it works!

Here are some questions to ponder that might jog your memory as to your impossible dream:

- What have you done in your life that seemed effortless, that you could spend hours doing and never realize the passage of time?
- When have you been so immersed in your activity that you lost track of time, felt no hunger, or fatigue? What were you doing at the time?
- If money were not an issue, what would you be doing right now, or how would you express your passion?
- Your brain does not know what it can't do until you tell it. What have you been telling your brain that it cannot do?

- Who would you like to inspire or assist? In what way? What is one step that you can begin right now to help this person?
- If you only had six months to live, how would you change your life or your mind?
- What inner urges have you had lately?
- What inner urges have you resisted in your life?

Answer these questions honestly and you will be closer to knowing your divine purpose.

If it feels good; if it feels right;
you are helping.

—Debbie Allen, International Speaker
and author of *Expert of Experts*

It is within you: the answers you seek,
the direction you want, and the power to be whoever
you want to be. Your dreams are not yours by mere
whim. They've been meticulously matched to the gifts
you're now developing. Designed to lure you within,
where your true power lies, and then out into
the world, beyond imagined limitations and fears.
Trust yourself. Listen to your heart. You have the right
stuff, you know what to do, and it can all be yours.

—Mike Dooley, *Notes from the Universe*

■

Chapter Two

Finding Your Passion and Taking Steps to Create It

The truth is, you can do or be anything you want, as long as you are willing to do the work. And what is the work? It is separating truth from fiction. In other words, dropping many of the *should* ideas you were taught and moving into your heart to discover your true and natural abilities, along with what you love doing.

Most people have been programmed with the idea that you *should* have a good job with a 401K, benefits, insurance, and longevity. This is a survival mentality. The focus is on how you are benefiting, rather than on what you are giving and expressing. Surviving is not about following your heart's desire and living a life of joy and passion.

It may be possible that you have been taught to go for work that is currently in demand right now. Get into a *good industry*. What is in demand? Teachers, engineers, computer technicians, nurses. It varies according to the time period. Yet, time passes and the next demand replaces the previous ones.

Perhaps you were instructed to follow in the family's footsteps. Everyone in your family is a business person, accountant, doctor, entrepreneur, or blue-collar worker. This may work for you or it may not.

These are the types of ideas that get in the way of connecting with the power of your spirit and acknowledging what you love. You can easily become misled and lost.

Here is a story to illustrate my point.

In one of his books, Dr. Norman Vincent Peale tells a story of a young man who followed his successful father into the insurance business and, subsequently, failed three times. While the young man conversed with Peale about his predicament, he gently, lovingly stroked the wood grain of a nearby table.

Peale commented on the young man's interest in the table, to which the man replied that he had always valued wood. He loved the textures, the feel of it. He enjoyed crafting beautiful wooden pieces. Peale suggested that he explore this passion to see what it might offer as a livelihood.

The young man eventually became quite successful in the design and manufacture of furniture. His pieces were remarkable and treasured as works of art. In giving up a business that did not suit him, this young man transformed from an inadequate insurance man to a talented, successful craftsman.

This fellow serves as an example for all of us in that everyone has genius and talent for something. Each person is unique in the same way that every snowflake is different and distinctive. By discovering your specific genius, you uncover your gift to the world and your path to fulfillment.

Rudolph Nureyev, the Great Russian ballet dancer, was passionate about his art. He said, "Work is sacred." The reason work was sacred to Nureyev was because he loved it. We must reach for the sacred as we seek the endeavor that will consume much of our lives. Loving what you do is key to living a life of joy and passion. That is what will guide you to fulfilling your impossible dream.

Our *highest* duty is to follow our bliss. From there, doing the impossible becomes natural. Zen calls it *the infinite way of doing finite things.*

The way we look at work sets the tone for how we deal with challenges and the way we pursue our dreams. It is relevant to moving forward passionately and reevaluating our position in life and our natural abilities. This is about becoming alive.

As the saying goes, *When you feel the bliss, there is no difficulty that is insurmountable. If you miss the bliss, there is no compensation adequate.*

The Process

The main thing is to get in touch with what is right for you. This idea may be considered indulgent, and it is. You are indulging your highest mental concept and your most profound aspirations. You will *never* be as successful as you could be until you get in touch with what is right for you in the same way Peale's client did.

Pay attention. This means doing what is *natural* for you. How do you discover what that is?

In truth, you have always known what is right for you. It has come through in every aspect of your life. You have always known what you love.

Here are some clues:
- What do you love to talk about?
- In what have you always been interested?
- What is/was your favorite sport or subject in school?
- What awards or achievements have given you the most pleasure?
- What are the things you do well without thinking about it?
- What games did you enjoy playing as a child?

- Who are the people you most admire and why?
- What fantasies have you had?
- What kinds of books do you enjoy reading?
- What are the things you dislike? This would be attacking the subject from the reverse angle and it works.

Following are some examples from people I have worked with.

When Diana was a child, she would find strips of different colored fabrics and hang them from the trees in her yard so she could watch the designs they created as the wind blew. Diana became a designer of rooms, houses, and all kinds of things.

As a youngster, Brenda liked to take big sheets of paper to draw houses and room arrangements. She eventually got into real estate, then worked for a not-for-profit housing developer who built multi-million dollar projects in Chicago. She was, indeed, drawing out buildings and configurations. Brenda was living her dream.

When I asked Garrett what games he loved to play as a child, he responded, "Cowboys." His passion for being a cowboy was rooted in his love for the wide-open range. That was his kingdom. Garrett decided to develop a lawn-care business where he could indulge his desire to be outside on the open range. Instead of riding a horse, he now rides a lawnmower.

Another client, Anise, loved food, food-preparation, menus, and nutrition. Anise started a catering business. She then pursued buying a bakery and becoming a dietician.

Katrina had a passion for detective stories when she was a child. She was intrigued with finding the right clues and solving the mystery. Working as a real-estate agent was a perfect fit for

Katrina because she got to figure out the clues as to what her buyers needed. She was able to come up with the exact right combinations to solve their mysteries and help them find their right homes.

All of these people had self-doubts about being good enough or qualified enough to attain their dreams. But as they recognized that the work they moved into matched their childhood passions, they understood they were being guided to their most natural expressions. Each was successful in their work.

Here are some folks you may recognize, along with what they have said about doing what they love.

Inventor Thomas Edison alleged he never worked a day in his life. He so loved what he did.

Comedian George Burns said, "Love what you do and you will stay young." He did his last show when he was 100 years old.

Computer genius Steve Jobs held that, "The only way to do great work is to love what you do."

The Mind Responds to Questions

When you ask a question, the mind begins to search for the answer. It is like a computer searching for the data that you request. Use questions to find the answers you seek. Here are some questions to help you uncover your outrageous dream,

- If in your wildest dreams, you could have anything you want, what would your life be like? Describe it.
- Describe predominant daydreams you have had throughout your life.
- What types of games did you play as a child? Dress up, fashion model, movie star, race-car driver, soldier, etc.?

- Passions: List the things you would do whether you were paid for doing them or not. These are things you can't wait to do.
- What things do you do for fun?
- What was the best vacation you ever had? Why?
- Describe a day that you felt was perfect. What made it perfect?

Study your answers to recognize patterns and repeated themes. Then, do these exercises to help you discover and reinforce what you love to do.

- Make a list of the things you thoroughly enjoy doing. Limit the list to those activities that inspire you at the mere thought of them. The shorter the list, the easier it is to reach the desired result.
- Select the item on the list that is most important to you. Do this, no matter how much you may resist picking one item. Selecting one does not mean that you have to give up doing the others forever.
- Make a list of the ways you can express the item or activity you selected in the second step. It is best to do this daily. Do not judge the ideas that come to you as you do this exercise. Write down every possibility that flows through your mind, no matter how silly or meaningless it may appear. The purpose of the exercise is to stimulate your creative mind. With daily contemplation, you will discover patterns and get clearer about how you can begin.
- Create a chart to identify your fantasies and inner urges using the example below.

  Column One: List fantasies, urges, and dreams that you entertain concerning work, career, and creativity. Visualize yourself doing what you've written. For instance, if you see yourself singing in a concert at Carnegie Hall, visualize it, feel what it would be like. An inspiration will come out of your visualization.

Column Two: Describe actions you can take to explore these dreams. Choose one or two and give them a try. In a month or two, check your list again and see if you want to try another option. Give yourself six months to a year to explore and discover what comes of your efforts.

Fantasies & Urges	Actions
Sing in a Concert at Carnegie Hall	Call local voice teachers, explore voice lessons.
	Pursue participation in choruses and/or singing groups.
	Purchase wordless music recordings and use them to practice singing .
Open a Book Store	Talk to people who own shops (of every kind) and find out what it takes to open and run a shop.
	Look for entrepreneurial classes at a nearby college.
	Learn the art of running a business from retired businessmen who volunteer at the Small Business Administration.
	Check the internet for free information on starting a business.

What is your dream? What activities would help you get started?

*Be easy about all of this. Life is supposed to be fun,
you know. It is Abraham's powerful desire that
you return to your state of self-appreciation.
We want you to feel love for your life, for the people
of your world, and most of all, for yourself.*
—Abraham, channeled through Esther Hicks

*Appreciation and self-love are the most important
tools that you could ever nurture. Appreciation of
others and the appreciation of yourself is the closest
vibrational match to your Source Energy of anything
that we've ever witnessed anywhere in the Universe.*
—Abraham, channeled through Esther Hicks

■

Chapter Three

Give Yourself Credit

Giving yourself credit is a profound and dynamic way to condition yourself for success. We have all tended to underestimate the power of the mind. Yet, there is no invention, organization, business, or anything worthwhile that did not start with an idea in someone's mind. This includes all art, music, architecture, technology, modes of transportation, and healing modalities. Everything starts as an idea.

To take this further, if you are to be your amazing outrageous self and do what seems to be impossible, you must start with your own self-assessment. As Henry Ford once said, "If you think you can or you think you can't, you are right." Learning how to think you *can* is crucial to being able to accomplish anything. That is the goal of this chapter: to help you build your self-esteem and confidence so that you *know* you can. The process involves five steps, each one requiring some action on your part.

Step One

The first step is to give yourself credit. All too often, people look at what they don't have, rather than what they do have.

"I don't have a college education or the right education."

"I don't know the right people."

"I don't have enough money."

"My parents won't like it."

These are *not-haves* and they are not important. What is important is what you do have.

Do you have determination, curiosity, courage, creativity, resourcefulness, inventiveness, motivation, openness, and willingness to learn? Do you manage challenge? Do you say *yes* to solving problems?

There is a societal tenet that you are not supposed to give yourself credit. Yet, that is the only way you will discover your talents and gifts. If you can't admit to your talents, you are stuck and going nowhere. This is a boundary you must cross. Certainly, no one knows your abilities better than you do.

One evening, I was conducting a class called "Developing Your Intuition," and a topic came up. It could have been on sensing someone's intent, or reading energy, or a variety of subjects. I made the comment, "Oh, I'm really good at that." For me, this meant that I had perfected that particular skill.

One of the male students responded, "And you are modest, too."

Take note, this is the type of criticism or judgment one encounters when they give themselves credit for a developed ability. For someone else, it could be, "I am good with numbers," or "I have a knack for decorating," or "I am a fast runner."

At break time, I approached the student who had expressed the sarcastic remark and asked him, "Do you have daughters?"

"Yes," he responded.

"Do you think it is a good idea for them to give themselves credit for a job well done, or do you think it would be better for them to be modest and keep quiet? Essentially, to hide their light under a bushel basket, so to speak."

"No, I want them to have confidence and believe in themselves. I want them to be able to honor their gifts and abilities."

I walked away, point made. My thought was, *Isn't it a shame that we, as a culture, have bought into the idea that it is not okay to honor oneself by admitting to our abilities?* This *modesty*, if you will, is one of the ways we block our Light and keep from moving forward. It is also why people don't get the jobs or careers they want. How can someone hire you if you can't tell them about your expertise. Most employers don't read minds.

Don't shortchange yourself. Give yourself credit so that others will know what you can do.

Another time, a student approached me and said, "I don't have any trouble finding people to talk to when I have failed at something, but I have no one with whom I can share my triumphs."

I told her, "Please call me when you want to share a success. I would love to hear about it."

And she did. We celebrated together.

Are you willing to celebrate others? If not, how can they celebrate you?

Step Two

The second step is to realize that everything you have done in your life has contributed to being who you are and will assist you in achieving the success you desire. Life is a series of steps.

Here is my story.

I got married young. I wanted to be independent and on my own, and that was the way you did it back then. I had four children who are now grown. I managed everything at home: all appointments for doctors and dentists, workmen installing windows and such, events, holidays, birthday parties. I paid the bills, made purchases for the household, planned and prepared meals, attended school conferences, gardened . . . you name it. I was everything implied by the term *household engineer.*

Motherhood, for me, involved volunteering as well. In that vein, I became a Girl Scout leader, Cub Scout leader, room mother, volunteer nurse, served on the PTA and various committees, wrote a *camping out* cookbook, and helped direct a day camp for kids. In other words, I developed leadership, teamwork, and communication skills.

Later, as I moved into my passion for metaphysics, I took classes, directed a metaphysics school, then more schools, then a whole region of schools, while I served on various boards of directors. I lectured, designed and taught classes, conducted leadership training, wrote articles and books, and did guest spots on television and radio shows. You might say my skills grew.

At some point, I was ready to be on my own and build my own business. As I got started, I used all the talents, creativity, and skills I had developed in all of my previous pursuits and applied them to my own vision of helping people.

I have always worked with people. As I began building my coaching and consulting business, I worked with universities, churches, and businesses. I designed and taught classes, provided over 35,000 Akashic (psychic) readings to people all over the world, had a syndicated radio show in 110 national markets, wrote columns for major newspapers in Saint Louis, and articles for publications all over the country. I worked with thousands of clients. You guessed it: I helped them become empowered and create their impossible dreams.

As you follow this chronology, you will note how my frame of reference grew. Yours will grow as well.

To get started on your story, go back to the list of clues given earlier and ask yourself some probing questions like, "What have I always loved doing?" Keep your mind open and listen to your heart. Soon, you will begin to receive guidance.

Life is a process, not a destination. We can learn from everything we do, whether we enjoy it or not, whether we are successful at it or not. Sometimes doing things badly helps guide just as much as doing things well. If you fail at adding or multiplication of numbers and discover that math is not your long suit, you may have saved yourself a lot of trouble, especially if accounting was on your career path. Remember how the inadequate insurance man became a great furniture maker?

Back to the process.

Playing golf is a process. Being a good musician is also a process. So is art, speaking, languages, teaching, technology, and just about everything. As you work in developing your process, your skills and confidence grow.

If you go into a golf game simply to win, you are out of control. You could be playing Tiger Woods, Ricky Fowler, or some other great golf wiz. If you enroll in a golf game to work on your swing, you are in control. Why? Because you can focus on improving your swing, no matter who you are playing. As your golf swing progresses, you become more skilled at the whole game. Pretty soon you are winning!

Just as golf is a process, life is also a process. Note this in the chronology of my personal development. Everyone is in a process of development. The key is to recognize and enjoy the process, not to focus on winning or any other outcome as a way to measure progress. If you keep working on the elements and skills required, you will eventually win at whatever you are doing. Keep practicing. Don't make a particular result the ultimate goal because, by working the process, you will advance, and thus, your target may change. Just keep practicing.

I have a brother-in-law named Phil. Just out of school, he started his career as a draftsman with a Saint Louis window company that designed, manufactured, and installed windows for large commercial buildings all over the world. Always creative, Phil grasped every opportunity offered at the company and grew his skill-set as he moved up the ladder. He ultimately designed buildings and the windows that went into them, became an executive and team leader, and traveled all over the world.

Later, he was offered the opportunity to buy the company he had worked at and helped grow all those years. Step-by-step, Phil went from a draftsman fresh out of school to owner of the company. He did the impossible. When he started out, he did not think he would eventually own the company. That part of his story came after years of learning, building skills, and growing in confidence. It was a natural outcome.

Step Three

The third step involves assessing your natural inclinations and desires. In other words, gather information by researching what is needed to accomplish your impossible dream. Are there people you can talk to who have insight or guidance? Are there books to read or workshops you can attend? Get out and talk to people and ask questions.

To help you with this, make sure the people in your life are *up-people* and not *down-people*. Make sure they want to see you succeed. Small-minded people love to watch folks fail. It justifies their lack of effort. Eliminate them from your life.

You aren't dependent on the world's opinions to accomplish what you want.

Generally, the world thinks inventive people who march to their own drumbeat are crackpots. In truth, what the world thinks of you or your process is none of your business. The world likes to judge on appearances. It has a very small frame of reference. Every time someone judges another person or idea, that person justifies his own lack. Successful people don't judge. They have no need to judge.

Step Four

The fourth step is to take one step at a time, be patient, and learn as you go. Make a plan but hold it loosely. As you move toward your desire, opportunities will present themselves. Take advantage of them. Don't worry about failure. It is a learning process. Each step gets you closer.

Here are some examples of people who didn't let tough times keep them down.

Thomas J. Watson, the founder of IBM, was no stranger to failure. Watson ran afoul of the antitrust laws and had been fired as the sales manager of the National Cash Register Company. At forty years of age, he was under a jail sentence, without a home or job, and had little money. Yet, even with this extraordinary pressure, he emerged to establish one of the most successful, innovative businesses in America.

A more current example of rags to riches takes form in J.K. Rowling, the author of the Harry Potter book series. From an early age, Rowling had ambition to be a writer. Little came from her early efforts. At age six, she wrote a book about a rabbit with measles, which her mother praised. That is when she decided she wanted to be a published author.

Rowling was living on State Benefits in England while writing her first Harry Potter book. It took a year for her agent to find a small publisher to publish the book. In 1996, the first book started to sell. By 2011, according to Britain's *Sunday Times Rich List,* her estimated wealth stood at millions of Euro. At that time, the global Harry Potter brand was estimated to be worth billions.

You might say Rowling never forgot her childhood goal. She states clearly that mistakes are important if you want to achieve success. Falling down helps us learn to pick ourselves up again. It is a valuable skill if you plan on doing the impossible.

Step Five

The fifth step requires awareness. Be aware. Make choices. Watch for opportunity.

Remember your credo that you can be, have, or do anything you want as long as you are willing to do the work. This means to be willing to render the internal and external changes you need to make. Give up negativity, victimhood, fear. Adopt courage, creativity, and innovation. Take the necessary risks. Be willing to grow.

Reverend Tom Johnson proclaimed, "Whatever we do to move ourselves into greater expression, the more we live, the more we have."

Oprah Winfrey stated, "God had a plan for me bigger than the one I had for myself."

We are radiant beings. It is our job to express our radiance in ways that enlarge our world.

Why You May Not Want to Know

As an aside, there are reasons why a person may not want to know what their life's work is, because knowing brings a responsibility to take action. See if you identify with any of the reasons listed here.

- If I don't know, I don't have to assume responsibility for taking action.
- If I don't know, I have an excuse for not doing it.
- If I don't know, I can't be blamed for not pursuing it or achieving it.
- If I don't know, I don't have to deal with other people's opinions.
- If I don't know, I don't have to take the chance of looking foolish.
- If I don't know, I don't have to step out of my comfort zone.
- If I don't know, I don't have to change.

Fear can interfere with achievement. This includes the fear of failure, fear of having to sacrifice something, fear of rejection, fear of reality, fear of making commitments, fear of making mistakes, fear of not being in control, or fear that it will not work. When fear overrides passion, nothing gets done.

Decide how you want your life to be. Create a plan at where you are right now, knowing that the plan will most likely change and grow as you grow. Then begin your journey with the first step.

I have given up the little self for the Holy Self and I have found the Way. I have wings as eagles, and into the heavens I have flown, a flight of joy and gladness that has taken me to the Secret Place on the Mountain, the very Kingdom of God. And here I run, and I am not weary; and I walk, and I do not faint. The Dawn is here. The Eagles are flying.

—John Randolph Price, Author

What is necessary to change a person is to change his awareness of himself.

—Abraham Maslow, Psychologist

If you know who you are, you cannot be offended.

—Jack Schwarz, Healer, Author, Teacher, Concentration-Camp Survivor

■

Chapter Four

Identity: I Am What?

An important lesson is to recognize how you identify or envision yourself. For instance, complete these statements with as many words as come to your mind in ten seconds.

- I am . . .
- I am . . .
- I am . . .
- I am . . .
- I am . . .

If you are not sure how to respond to this assignment, look at your behavior. How do treat yourself? Do you drag yourself out of bed each morning with a groan? Another dreary day? Do you grab coffee and a donut to get yourself moving?

On the other hand, perhaps you begin the day with an energy drink and granola bar. You leave your house excited with a plan for the day.

How does your behavior define you? Do you see life as an adventure or a drag? If someone were observing your words and actions, how would that person perceive you?

"She is energized."

"He is loving."

"She is bored."

"He is boring."

How you define yourself is important question because the way you identify yourself is what you give to the world. It is what you end up with as well. If you are not aligned with what you wish to achieve and project, change the way you define yourself. There is no limit to what you can become and accomplish, but it is up to you. It all starts with the way you identify yourself.

All my life, as I researched successful people, I questioned how destiny fell to each one. These were the people who freed the slaves, discovered electricity, invented the telephone, rode through villages on a horse to warn the people the British were coming. As I read their stories, my questions were, "How did they get there? How did they know what to do and how to do it? How did they know?" These were stories of presidents, inventors, scientists, patriots, designers, land owners, diplomats, and writers.

Another way to ask about these successful people might be this: "How did they define themselves? How did they decide that they were to be a president, a diplomat, a patriot, a designer, a spy, or an inventor?"

Most of us were instructed by others, positively and/or negatively, in our identities.

"You're great at math."

"You will never amount to anything."

"You really catch on quickly."

"You are a great athlete."

" You don't know what you are doing?"

Good or bad, who told you this and why did you decide to listen?

It is easy to hear people define themselves.

"No one in my family has a college education."

"Everyone in my family is a doctor or a professional."

What are your family dynamics? What was the message you were given? Do you still carry it?

Occasionally, I meet someone who informs me that they were raised with the idea they could do anything, and they accepted it. That is unusual and fantastic. I would love it if everyone had that type of indoctrination. What if you decide that, right now, you are incredibly capable of accomplishing whatever you want and that is your new mantra and identity? "I can accomplish anything."

This means you will need to follow up with behaviors that match this new self-concept. Try new things, educate yourself in new areas and subjects, challenge yourself, stretch your boundaries every day.

Many people are lazy and won't challenge the things they were taught. Are you happy with the stories you were told? Are these good enough for you? What are your own personal standards? Do you need to raise them?

I had a business partner, Josephine, who was instructed by her elementary school teacher, "You will never be good at math!" The teacher spoke this with great venom. Thus, when anything came up that had to do with mathematics, finances, or accounting, Josephine would disintegrate into a pile of nerves. She totally bought into the idea that she could not be adequate at anything pertaining to math. Yet, when we were business associates, she managed two business accounts for her husband, as well as the books for our business, without incident or problem. I asked her why she would want to accept the inane pronouncements of a frustrated schoolteacher to limit her progress in life?

Along the same lines, your progress and success coordinates perfectly with your identity. When you say, "I am sick, tired, excited, inspired, motivated, disgusted," you live it. Once you speak your words, every energy in the Universe magnetizes to fulfill your decision. Decide carefully and align your actions with your words.

Abraham, channeled through Esther Hicks, said, "When someone offers you a negative thought or you're offering yourself one, say 'Thank you. That is not part of my vision,' and move on. Don't give it another thought. This is described as your conscious mind being an ant walking on the back of your subconscious mind, which is the size of an elephant. You want your ant and your elephant to be moving in the same direction. Your subconscious mind is always going in the right direction, but your conscious mind, where your thoughts lie, will offer you negativity and take you out of alignment. Don't let the ant choose your direction."

The action I observed with the people I researched, including people like Paul Revere, George Washington, John Adams, Abigail Adams, Abraham Lincoln, Ben Franklin, George Washington Carver, and Oprah Winfrey, illustrated their identity as "I am inspired. I am willing. I am able. I am focused."

The question then is what have you accepted as your current identity and *when* did you make that decision? Like Josephine, did you resolve this when you were seven years old, or ten, or sixteen, or as an adult? Do you passionately desire to change it in order to be kinder, more thoughtful, healthier, stronger, a great partner, an amazing parent or friend, or to be more inspired? What action do you resolve to do daily to bring about this result? If you aren't acting it out, you have not yet claimed it. The sky is the limit, but you have to do the work.

It breaks down like this: You have two selves. One is eternal and unchangeable and the other is changeable and contrived. The first is brilliant, beautiful, inventive, creative, and loving.

The other is fabricated out of the ideas you have adopted, accepted, and invented. Your eternal self is always present underneath the surface. The more you identify with that self, the greater will be your expression, determination, and creativity. That self is unstoppable.

Most people identify with their fabricated self, which permits others' views of them to determine how they feel about themselves. So, if someone thinks you are unlikeable or incompetent, you may believe them.

There was a group of challenged students who were considered slow-learners, behind in comprehension as compared to their same-grade counterparts. For some reason, the teacher assigned to this class was erroneously informed that these students were high achievers. She proceeded to teach then from that point of view. No one corrected her as no one knew of the mistake. At the end of the school year, the supposedly *slow* students were ahead in comprehension to the normal kids. The teacher saw them as accelerated and treated them as such. They took on that identity.

If someone told you that you are stupid or ugly, would you decide to believe them? What if they said you were incompetent or a loser? Or would you accept the idea that you are brilliant, innovative, awe-inspiring, and creative? If I told you that you have green hair, would you believe that? You can see by these questions that people often tell you the most outrageous things. However, you are the ultimate judge as to what makes sense to you.

People project their insecurities onto others, as in the case of the frustrated school teacher who told Josephine she would never be good at math. As you realize that others' words are about them and not you, you relax, knowing what they think has nothing to do with you. You are the designer of your own identity.

Author Richard Bach says it this way. "If your happiness depends on what somebody else does . . . you do have a problem."

Once you are clear as to who you are and have dedicated yourself to a positive self-portrayal, you will become impervious to insults or offense. When you are certain of your intelligence, someone else's conclusion that you aren't bright means nothing to you. In fact, you would look at the person as though he had two heads. Of course, you are not stupid. You are brilliant. Know this. Immediately, you understand that your accuser has a perception problem or perhaps he is frustrated and doesn't know any better. In that case, you would feel bad for him and let his remark slide off your back. Clearly he is confused and projecting his own problem on to you.

The Course in Miracles states this principle. "Projection makes perception. The world you see is what you gave it, nothing more than that. But though it is no more than that, it is not less. . . . It is the witness to your state of mind, the outside picture of an inward condition. As a man thinketh, so he perceives."

When I was a child about seven years old, I was informed that I was born in sin. I thought that was the stupidest idea I had ever heard. How can a baby be born in sin? *Crazy!* I dismissed the whole thing and thought the person that stated it must be a little nuts.

This is called discrimination. You are to discriminate what makes sense to you. Are you brilliant and God-created? Who are you? How have you identified yourself?

*Aerodynamically, the bumblebee shouldn't
be able to fly, but the bumblebee doesn't know it
so it goes on flying anyway.*

—Mary Kay Ash, Founder of Mary Kay Cosmetics, Inc.

*Consult not your fears, but your hopes and
your dreams, Think not about your frustrations,
but about your unfulfilled potential.
Concern yourself not with what you tried
and failed in, but with what it is still
possible for you to do.*

—Pope John XXIII, Theologian

■

Chapter Five

Victims Stay Small,
Innovators Soar with the Eagles

Victims can be very beguiling because, mostly, they are sweet people-pleasing people. For those reasons, they look inviting. You like their sincerity. However, victims do not have a self. They look externally for their good and tend to take everything personally. "How come people aren't nice to me? Why do I always get the short end of the stick?"

The reason they don't get the goodies is because they do not love and credit themselves with their brilliance and magnificence. Instead, they look to others to wave their banner. They end up waiting in the wings. "When is it my turn? When does my number come up?"

They don't understand that it is up to them to create their adventure and success. Their tendency is to look at what is wrong, rather than what is right. Because of this, they end up creating more of what they don't want.

The truth is that victims are stuck. They cannot get what they want by looking for others to fix their problems. They must learn to empower themselves, to take command so that they can live their lives in triumph.

Here are some rules for empowerment.

Empowerment Rule 1: Take full responsibility for your life. You may not be able to control all your circumstances, but you have total control on how you respond to them.

Actor and businessman Arnold Schwarzenegger is a perfect example of someone who chooses his reactions to circumstances. Schwarzenegger was born in a rural Austrian town in 1947. His family home was basic, without indoor plumbing or electricity. He and his brother walked a long distance to bring buckets of water home for cooking and bathing. There were no paved roads in his little town. Yet, none of this played into Arnold's plan for his life. His dreams started when he first saw cowboy movies. That was when he decided that he was going to be a movie star.

By the age of twenty, Schwarzenegger dominated the sport of competitive bodybuilding to become the youngest person ever to win the Mr. Universe title. His first gym was a simple tree limb on which he did chin-ups. He concocted other outdoor exercises to build his physique before he was able to work out in a gym. The sport of bodybuilding is what catapulted him into the public's eye. He used it to create fame and reputation.

When he made it to the United States, he worked in gyms and training facilities and wrote fitness manuals, which he sold from his home. He started investing in Los Angeles real estate. He bought a small apartment building and lived in one apartment while he let the rent from the other units pay for the building.

Through his bodybuilding activities, he met many people in the movie business and, ultimately, started acting in movies. He kept his eyes on his goals and became a top-grossing movie star. He used his fame and business acumen to become the governor of California.

Schwarzenegger was never afraid of hard work. Nor did he limit himself due to not having money, to knowing the right people, or to background, cultural, and language issues,. He took control of himself and looked for opportunity. The circumstances and deprivations that might have stopped others were never considered. He kept his focus, grasping each opportunity to move toward his desire. He understood that, if you want something, there is a way for you to have it. He was outrageous in his work ethic and routinely did what others would consider impossible.

His story is a reminder that dreams really can come true if you supply the effort. When you let external conditions control your destiny, you surrender your power and authority. By the same token, when you allow someone else to be in charge of your life, you keep yourself stuck. If you believe that others are responsible for your loss or failure, it follows that they are the powerful ones and you are not. You are a mere victim. Blaming and feeling helpless or sorry for yourself wastes time and energy. These are bad choices.

Take control of your life by setting your own standards, taking responsibility, and being what you want to be. Next time you face an occasion to lose your cool, stop and reflect. Consider the option of remaining calm. Let go of any learned inclination toward anger, resentment, jealousy, or violence. Instead, decide how you would like to feel. With practice, you can establish an inner space of unflinching peace, impervious to the whims of others.

Empowerment Rule 2: Don't arbitrarily accept someone else's beliefs and opinions. A belief is a thought that has been repeated over and over. This is an important point because it implies that you can create new beliefs and repeat them until you own them.

For example, you can change an old belief like, "I'm nobody," to "I love that I am unique."

Often, we are around people and institutions that proliferate certain messages. You can easily become indoctrinated. Think about the glazed looks on the faces of the German people in those World War II videos when Hitler was railing about his vision for world domination. His fervor and determination transferred to them and they became his robots, carrying out his concept for a *perfect race* while the country fell apart and millions were murdered.

Frequently, people adopt beliefs that make no logical sense and do not resonate to their true selves. Learn to listen to your heart. If your heart or gut doesn't feel good with a belief, then it is not true for you. Your soul is always speaking to you. Listen to it.

Empowerment Rule 3: If you need to do it, do it. That means leave a miserable job or relationship, relocate, or start over.

Do you remember the story of Colonel Harlan Sanders of Kentucky Fried Chicken fame? He closed his Fried Chicken Restaurant in Kentucky when he was sixty-two and started selling franchises. In 1964, when he was seventy-four, he had more than 600 franchised outlets, which he then sold to a group of investors for $2 million. The point? At any time or age, you can begin again.

Your life is your journey. Don't let it become your rut. If you are not growing, do something different. Make a change. Let go. Move on.

Empowerment Rule 4: The saying goes, "God does not make junk." In other words, you are valuable. Remind yourself daily. Talk to yourself out loud and affirm your value.

As a child, Academy Award-winning filmmaker Brian Grazer was informed that he was not a good student. This occurred at a time before *learning disorders* were diagnosed. He was programmed with the idea that he was not smart. His report cards reinforced this as well. His saving grace was his grandmother, who readily reminded him that he was special.

The *2007 Entertainment Weekly's "The 50 Smartest People in Hollywood"* listed Glazer as Number 11. So much for not being smart! Also in 2007, Grazer was chosen by *Time Magazine* as one of the *100 Most influential People in the World.*

Brian Glazer credits his success to curiosity. Throughout his life, he turned his insatiable curiosity to connecting with people and learning their stories. These stories inspired his award-winning movies and television shows.

He comments, "I like learning stuff. The more information you can get about a person or a subject, the more you can pour into a potential project. I made a decision to do different things, I want to do things that have a better chance of being thought of as original. I do everything I can to disrupt my comfort zone."

Glazer outlined his use of curiosity in his book, *A Curious Mind: The Secret to a Bigger Life.* Glazer has made movies and television programs for more than twenty-five years. Over his career, his movies and television shows have been nominated for a total of fifty-two Oscars and ninety-four Emmys. His movies have generated more than $13.5 billion in worldwide theatrical, musical, and video grosses.

Consequently, if you start doubting your worth, remember Brian Glazer. He did not let his teacher's opinion define him. Glazer admittedly loves challenging himself and the results are tangible.

What you focus on increases. Therefore, focus on your worth and it will increase.

Empowerment Rule 5: If you want to do something, do it. Your soul is calling to you. When you over-think every decision, you end up standing still. It is called analysis paralysis. As Nike says, "Just do it!"

You want to change jobs? Do it. You want to make new friends? Do it. You want to learn a new skill? Do it. You want to travel? Figure out a way and do it.

Empowerment Rule 6: Do the work and get rid of your emotional baggage. This includes memories of being hurt, offended, or criticized. Let it go! So your mother didn't love you enough and your father wasn't there? That is on them and not you. Forgive them and move on. Also, forgive your brother, your sister, your mean-spirited boss, your soccer coach, your junky neighbors, and the rude store clerk. Let them all go. Don't give up any mental space for animosity. As you let go, you will feel the weight coming off your shoulders and you will feel free. You are free to experience peace, even when living in a chaotic environment.

In his book, *Man's Search for Meaning*, Viktor Frankl, a survivor of Auschwitz, stated that, no matter what his captors did to him, they could not control his mind. In his mind, Frankl held visions of being home with his wife. He also chose to avoid opportunities to hate his captors, but directed his imagination to sweet memories of home. Consequently, Frankl was one of few prisoners to survive the concentration camp. He ultimately manifested his dream of returning home.

Empowerment Rule 7: Find a way to express yourself. Build something. Write something. Learn to draw or speak. Do something creative. Everyone needs an outlet to express energy, one that is uniquely one's own. Experiment until you discover yours. If you can't figure it out, take classes until you discover a way that feels good for you. You don't have to be a Picasso to paint or a Mark Twain to write. Just do it.

Empowerment Rule 8: Become a possibility-thinker. When you look at a person, relationship, or opportunity, ask yourself: What are the possibilities? Most people don't see the possibilities because they never ask the question. You must *seek* possibilities.

In his book, *How to Sell Anything to Anybody*, author Joe Girard, "The World's Greatest Salesman" of Michigan, saw possibility with every person he met and every name in the phone book. That included his dry cleaners, florist, barber, gas station attendant, etc. That is how he broke the record for car sales every year and became the greatest salesman.

Possibility-thinking must be cultivated. There are endless ways to accomplish anything, and circumstances do not dictate anyone's potential for success. Your parents or friends may have done something a certain way, but that does not mean you have to do it the same way. That requires opening your mind so that you, too, can do the impossible.

Think of it this way: You want a car. Most people would go to a car dealership, make arrangements, and purchase a car. That is one way to obtain a car. Other possibilities would be that you could inherit a car, win a car, be given a car, trade something for a car, be paid with a car, build your own car, or be supplied a car through your company. There could be a fire-sale on cars, or hail-damaged cars could be offered at ridiculously discounted prices. You could get a Nissan, Ford, Chevrolet, Kia, Toyota, Lexus, Saturn, Volkswagen, Jaguar, BMW, Mercedes, Jeep, Geo, E-car, station wagon, van, convertible, sports car, sedan, or truck. These are a few options.

The idea is that whether looking for a car, job, friend, house, college, mentor, book, or class, there are endless possibilities. The more you are able to recognize them, the easier it is to not limit yourself by smallness or tradition.

It takes patience, perseverance, and faith to develop possibility-thinking, but it can be done. Quantum physics teaches that we live in a field of energy in which a myriad of possibilities exist. This fits with our idea of getting a car. In physics, it is noted that the possibility you focus on, or register in your mind, is the one you choose. That means you get what you focus on. Another way to say it is that you are responsible for your result. Once you begin thinking about it, imagining it, and focusing on your idea, you are responsible for it. You want a job that supplies a car, or you go to the dealership and buy one. Where is your focus?

Chinese philosopher Chuang-tse tells the story of a great bird known as the P'eng. It had a back, broad as a mountain range that extended to support expansive wings, which swept the sky like clouds. In flight, the P'eng rose powerfully, like a whirlwind penetrating the high mist. It majestically soared into the heavens.

As the P'eng glided smoothly, effortlessly on its way to the sea, a quail in the marsh gazed up and laughed. "What does that bird think it is doing?" the quail exclaimed. "I leap, fly a few feet, and descend again. I flutter busily among the bushes, jumping from here to there and back again. That is what flying is for! Who is that creature trying to fool?"

In this example, you see the difference between a small thinker and one who chooses to soar. Small minds, lacking knowledge and perspective, do not lift their vision to comprehend greatness anymore than the words of a fool can equal the depth of a wise one, or the experience of a few years can equal that of many.

Remember this when the voice of inspiration speaks to you, and you recognize that it is time to step beyond past limitations because something greater beckons you. The creative among us can discern true art, the visionary can ascertain direction, and the small-minded will stand back in a safe domain and condemn.

Empowerment Rule 9: Turn failure into triumph. The loss of a job becomes the opportunity to find a better one or start a business. The completion of a relationship can mean you have grown or learned a lesson. It can lead you to new people, different opportunities, discovery of innovative experiences, and generally, freshen your life.

When Frederick Smith outlined his idea for an overnight delivery service, his Yale professor told him, "The concept is interesting and well-formed, but in order to earn a better grade than a C, it must be feasible." The professor felt that Smith had relied too much on the aviation industry in his design, causing his idea to be flawed and impractical. Smith did not let his C-grade stop him, and fortunately, he ignored his teacher's comments. He went on to found Federal Express. The rest is history.

The moral of the story is *get moving*. Don't let anyone tell you your idea won't work. Determine your goal and find a way around, through, or over every obstacle. Remember Arnold Schwarzenegger started with nothing. He built a real estate empire and a dynamic acting career by maintaining focus.

Not only do victims stay small, they keep themselves from following the soul's urge to do the impossible, to soar with the P'eng or the eagles.

Here are some questions to help you decide where you are in your process.

- Are you a victim or visionary?
- In what areas do you play the victim?
- In what areas are you the visionary?
- What is your greatest vision?
- Is it time to step into a vaster experience?
- What opportunities do you see or what opportunities are you willing to create?
- What would you be willing to risk in order to achieve your greatest desire?

*We should never lose sight of the fact that
the soul is on the pathway of an endless and
ever-expanding experience, and that only by expansion
can it evolve. Accepting the lessons and experiences
of the past and taking the best from everything,
we should press boldly forward, looking ever for
the Truth, and ever-ascending higher and
higher into the heavens of reality.*
—Ernest Holmes, Writer and Teacher

*Argue for your limitations, and sure enough,
they are yours.*
—Richard Bach, Author of *Illusions*

■

Chapter Six

Putting the Past in Proper Perspective

Setting up a pattern of doing the impossible requires new behaviors and habits. Living unconsciously keeps you stuck in
the same low-level energy with the same uninspiring outcomes.
For this reason, it is important to examine the past and put it in
proper perspective. It is a primary source of enlightenment. We
can get a handle on it by processing past beliefs and behaviors
so we are moving on to a more progressive future. Doing the impossible requires looking forward. Taking the gems from the past
with us makes it easier. This is similar to Edison stating that having
5000 failures in producing the light bulb, helped him find the
right way to make it work.

A space vehicle is propelled by rockets that fire in a programmed sequence in much the same way as each of us is propelled along life's journey by other people or events that influence us. Sometimes these influences are profoundly positive and
create major transitional moments. We look back at them as land-
marks on the terrain of our lives. Other times, the person or event
may appear negative or ominous. Yet, all serve as catalysts to bring
about the change required at the time. They all help us to move
along our path, just like the rocket.

Everyone can recall events that were turning points and individuals who effected transformation. Your parents obviously fit

this category. They provided your first boost into this world and their impact stayed with you. As their influence waned, the next *rocket* may have been a friend or teacher, and the next rocket, a spouse or mentor. Each person provided the exact encounter necessary to keep you progressing. Some people and events you welcomed gratefully and others caused you to cringe.

Whether a birth or a death, a promotion or divorce, each shaped and molded your character, your understanding, and your wisdom. These occurrences are neutral. Your reaction determines how they impact your life, whether they detract or add value. You choose how you view these events in the same way that you choose how they affect you. You experience gratitude or become somber, humble, or bitter.

For example, you are released from a job. You can see it as a doorway to another more exciting career, or you can spiral into victimhood. The choice on how to view the situation is yours.

A driver cuts in front of you as you navigate through traffic. A humble person might recognize the driver as panicked or in trouble. He might get out of the way to make room so the other driver can be on his way. Someone else might judge the incident intrusive and decide to compete for the road.

The first person does not take the incident personally and remains peaceful. The second one sees it as a personal affront and reacts with anger. In this case, the event colors his day. He will take his response with him wherever he goes. It will touch his interactions throughout the day. It will not add value. It will, instead, diminish him. And so it is with life. We choose to be enriched or diminished.

Can you remember the end of a relationship? Were you grateful for having had the experience? Or were you mad that it had ended? If you think of it as a completed phase of your life, would you judge it differently?

Attachment creates pain. When you have not processed an experience for its inherent blessing, you are attached to it and you are obliged to repeat it. Moving on in appreciation prepares you for the next opportunity. Appreciation is a high energy that expands your potential and keeps you excited and growing.

When we judge a situation negative, we vow not to do it again. This is not processing the experience. It is the reason why people who have had difficult marriages pledge never to marry again and think that solves the problem. It is the reason someone will replicate the same relationship pattern again and again.

For example, Jenny repeatedly got involved with alcoholics who brought chaos into her life. She couldn't understand how she was able to find the lone alcoholic in a room full of people, or why she kept attracting the same energy over and over. If she were to examine it closely, she would discover that picking alcoholics was a comfortable pattern for her. She knew what to expect. She could predict the chaos they brought with them. With awareness and self-discipline, Jenny could recognize her pattern and change this habit.

When people resolve never to do it again, they believe that avoidance or blaming it on someone or something else takes care of the matter. The problem is that the past energy is still alive. The situation or involvement has not been understood and forgiven.

Therefore, what is unresolved in you is still alive in you. You cannot dismiss it or ignore it until you have understood it. By giving it value, you can receive its transformative quality. This is the way you can use the past to create an expanded, positive future and reach your desired outcome. Doing the impossible requires it.

When Jenny acknowledges her unhealthy pattern of associating with alcoholics, she will gain the power to make new choices that lead to harmony. That is when she can use her newfound peace to accomplish amazing things.

Blaming and guilt trigger thoughts that encourage quick categorizing and dismissal. Blamers don't want to take responsibility for the course of their lives. Yet, blaming sets them up for more of the same. Understanding the dynamics of the past, will help them set up new methods and possibilities.

By developing a system founded on self-discipline, you will be able to put aside automatic, programmed reactions that are based on unrealistic expectations. Stop and assess a situation. What really happened? How did you draw this to you? What is the blessings? Self improvement is a worthy goal.

A sincere commitment to grow and a willingness to look honestly at the past will help you discern significance. "How have I changed as a result of this event? Or how can I change for the better?" In this way, you will envision the opportunity in the chaos.

Gerard is a great example of someone who made a firm commitment to advance beyond his past relationship issues. With each partner, he would give his all. Over time, each companion grew discontent, demanding more and more. It was a pattern. He might tell you that he had a number of failures, but you will see that is not a correct assessment.

When I explored this subject with Gerard, it was clear that he went out of his way to try to make his partners happy. He traced his behavior back to his mother, who seemed to require a lot of attention. With his mom, he found that, no matter what he did, she would not be happy. No matter what he did, he could not get her to be happy. He did not realize that being happy is a *choice*. Because he was never able to convert his mom to being happy, it felt like failure.

Gerard had transferred this pattern to his romantic interests. He unerringly picked partners that matched his mother's demands. When he realized that his repeated behavior was based on the erroneous idea that it was *his job* to please his mother and, likewise, the women in his life, he was able to make a change.

Gerard sought compatibility. By looking at his actions, he understood his patterns and the erroneous beliefs that went with them. He gave up on the idea that it was his job to please anyone. He learned to give without waiting to be acknowledged, and he sought partners that wanted reciprocity. Both gave and both received. This new approach offered balance, a shared experience, and more joy.

Striving for a broader perspective leads to freedom. Pain is relative. Generally, the most painful occurrences trigger the greatest growth. Often, it is through pain that we break free from unconscious assumptions, old beliefs, having to be right, wanting to look good, or struggling for approval.

Look for the value in an experience and you will find it. Each phase of your life will be perceived as a valued part of the continuum, and you will be prepared to move to more elevated heights of accomplishment.

As an exercise, contemplate what you can take from the stories in this chapter: Jenny who kept attracting the same person in different forms and Gerard who wanted to *make* his mother and the women in his life happy.

Failure: What is it?

The whole idea of failure is a fluke. There is no failure. There is trying and not trying.

People have a lot of misconceptions about failure. John Keats said, "Failure is, in a sense, the highway to success, inasmuch as every discovery of what is false leads us to seek earnestly after what is true." Keats is referring to the Law of Failure. It states that your level of success is directly proportional to how often you fail.

Everyone at some point deals with failure. If we let failing at something defeat us, we are in for a succession of depleting experiences.

Albert Einstein failed in his college entrance exams. Abraham Lincoln failed in business twice, was repeatedly defeated for public office, and had a nervous breakdown. Imagine the impact on the world if either of these great men decided to quit.

As a kid, Evander Holyfield fought another kid and lost. He went home and told his mother.

She said, "Go out there and fight him again."

He went out and fought the kid again and lost again.

When he got home, his mother said, "Get out there and fight him again."

Holyfield fought the kid four times. On the fourth time, he won.

What did he learn? He learned to observe his opponent and discern his weaknesses so that he could use this to his advantage. He learned valuable information from his early losses.

Few people know that when Jim Carrey, the famous comedic actor, was fourteen years old, he told his dad he wanted to be a comedian. His father took him to perform in a comedy club and Carrey was laughed off the floor. It didn't stop him because he has become a top-earning comedic movie actor. He has found his venue in film.

More currently, Joe Girard, the "World's Greatest Salesman" per *The Guinness Book of World Records,* had many failures. He was terrible as a sixteen-year-old thief and bad at holding jobs. He lost all his money in the construction business. When he got into car sales, however, Joe used all his past experiences, his penchant for keeping records, and his charismatic personality to excel. His first year out, he sold the most cars at the Detroit dealership where he worked. Every year after that, he beat his own record.

With every venture, there is an element of risk. Risk that you won't succeed at your intended goal. You take a job, for instance. It could be a fun, productive job or a nightmare. You travel on vacation. You could have a blast or the airline could lose your luggage, the hotel could cost twice as much as you had planned, and the food could be bad. Either way, you choose how you want to feel about the experience, take what you learned from it, and move on.

If you end up hating your job, it doesn't mean you are never to have another good job. It indicates you may have evaluated your talents, the boss, or the company incorrectly. Or it could mean things in the company changed midstream. Giving up is not the answer.

The idea with failure is that *you* are the failure. That is not true. That is the way the ego would interpret the experience.

We come into this world knowing nothing. The whole experience is trial-and-error. We take a step forward and discover what happens, what the consequences are. Based on that information, we take another step. No matter how calculating a person is, there are always surprises and unanticipated events. The point is, learn from everything. Keep gathering information. In time, you will accrue enough experience to gain more than you lose.

People think the success of a project is the goal. In reality, the evolution of the person is the goal. With the advantage of time and experience comes the wisdom to grow, to develop capabilities, expertise, and steel-like determination, and to keep going, no matter what. That is the definition of a victor.

There is no failure because external outcomes are unpredictable. You cannot fail because, by doing and trying and learning, you grow. That is the real possibility. *You* are the project and you cannot fail.

Even if you decide you hate your job, that is great information that helps you discover the kind of work you will love. If you realize you have no aptitude for language or technology, that awareness helps you eliminate those areas as career choices and narrows the field for something better suited for you.

Falling down helps us learn to pick ourselves up again. It is a valuable and necessary skill if you plan on succeeding.

Decide how you want your life to unfold. Create a plan, starting from where you are right now to where you want to be, knowing that the plan will change as you grow. Begin your journey with the first step. If one phase of your plan doesn't work, step back and reassess. Develop strategies as you go. Don't let rejection, failure, criticism, falling down, or anything else stop you. Take time daily to consider your current position and where you are headed. This clears your mind and creates room for new ideas. Remember the story of Arnold Schwarzenegger. He took many steps to ultimate success.

Concentrate on your desire. Make sure you are clear about desire and intent. Confused or fuzzy goals cannot be achieved.

Most importantly, don't get attached to how you achieve your result. Be willing to discern the ways that don't work so you can move closer to the ways that do. Like Thomas Edison, Walt Disney, Jim Carrey, and Joe Girard, stick to your goal. You will make *failure* a meaningless, obsolete word.

The only real failure is not trying at all.

No Excuses

Excuses keep you stuck. The only way you can live fully and tap into your genius self is by taking total responsibility for your life. That means no excuses, blaming, or finger-pointing.

When you plant lettuce, if it does not grow well, do you blame the lettuce? No, you look for reasons why it is not doing well. It may need fertilizer, more water, or less sun. You never blame the lettuce. Yet, if you have problems with your friends and family, you have a tendency to blame the other person.

Blaming has no positive effect, nor does trying to persuade someone to change by using reason and arguments. Look to yourself and determine what the issue is that overrides having a good connection? What part do you play and how to you want to address it? Answering these questions will pinpoint the problem. Determining how you want to change so that you don't let anyone else's behavior or beliefs keep you from being your amazing self, is the way to experience happiness. No blaming, no reasoning, no arguments, just understanding.

In *Peace Is Every Step,* Thigh Nhat Hahn says, "If you understand, and you show that you understand, you can love, and the situation will change."

Joe, who worked all day, found himself exasperated when he wanted to accomplish a project at home. His stay-at-home wife,

Amelia, constantly interrupted him. It was almost impossible to get anything done.

One day, it occurred to him that Amelia was home all day with little kids and needed an outlet to talk. So, he changed his attitude. When she approached him for a conversation, he set aside his tools and listened. With purposeful focus, she was able to have the adult outlet she craved. After about an hour, Amelia would be satisfied and Joe was able to go back to his project. Instead of blaming her or resorting to anger, Joe chose to understand her need and respond to it. The result was a happier marriage.

Thinking about *no excuses*, Kyle Maynard comes to mind. Maynard not only made no excuses for his disabilities, he routinely did the impossible. He was born March 24, 1986, with a condition known as congenital amputation. His arms ended at the elbows and his legs ended near the knees. His parents, Scott and Anita, made an important decision early-on to encourage their disabled son to be as independent as possible. Kyle refers to this as his *pursuit of normalcy*. As a result of his drive, he types up to fifty-words-per-minute with two elbows, eats and writes without adaptations, drives a car with little modification, and lives in his three-level townhouse in Atlanta, Georgia.

As an eleven-year-old, Maynard was determined to wrestle. He found a coach that gave him a chance to try. In the beginning, he lost every match, but that was only the beginning. Maynard, with his iron determination and supportive parents, started winning. In his senior year, he won thirty-six varsity matches. In his quest, he defeated several state place-finishers and state champions.

At the same age, Kyle began weight training. Eventually, he attained the title *GNC's World's Strongest Teen*. He did this by bench-pressing twenty-three repetitions of 240 pounds. In February, 2009, with the assistance of leather straps and chains attached to his arms, he successfully lifted 420 pounds.

Maynard's triumphs extend far beyond wrestling and weight-lifting. He was proclaimed the *2004 ESPY Award winner*— Best Athlete with a Disability—and a year later was inducted into the *National Wrestling Hall of Fame.* In 2007, he was elected by the U S Jaycees as one of the *Top Ten Outstanding Young Americans.* In 2008, Maynard received the *Highest Recognition Award of the Secretary of Health and Human Services* for his efforts as a life role-model, motivational speaker, and humanitarian.

In April, 2009, Kyle became the first quadruple amputee to compete as an amateur mixed-martial-arts fighter. He focused on grappling and ground fighting.

Another astounding achievement occurred with Kyle being the first man to climb on all fours to the 19,340-foot summit of Mount Kilimanjaro, the highest mountain in Africa. His companions on this climb were two Marine veterans who struggled through their own incredible adversities to reach the peak. They gave a powerful message to veterans and kids with disabilities: No disability is too great to be overcome. Kyle works with wounded soldiers on adapting their fitness regimens to meet their needs with a more functional methodology.

In 2008, Kyle brought life to one of his most fervent dreams. He built and opened his first fitness center, No Excuses CrossFit. His inspiring book, *No Excuses: The True Story of a Congenital Amputee Who Became a Champion in Wrestling and in Life,* is a New York Times bestseller. Kyle Maynard is a motivational speaker, author, entrepreneur, and athlete.

His story puts much into perspective. When we find ourselves too tired, too unmotivated, too anything that keeps us from moving forward, just remember Kyle Maynard and make no excuses.

Here is what he has to say about achieving dreams. "I've always believed that anyone can achieve their dreams, regardless. I've always had this attitude about no excuses. A belief that I can go on and do what I need to do. To go on, to succeed, regardless."

Have you made excuses and kept yourself from growing? If so, what were they? What would you like to do about it?

The master has failed more times than
the beginner has even tried.
—Stephen McCranie, Author and Cartoonist

Your task is not to seek for love,
but merely to seek and find
all the barriers within yourself
that you have built against it.
—Jalaluddin Rumi, Persian Poet, Sufi Mystic

■
Chapter Seven

No Put-Downs!

Negative energy is depleting. In this chapter, we will cover put-downs and self-destructive critical behaviors. Both have to become big No-No's.

Here is a story about a writer, John Kennedy Toole, who penned a comic novel, *A Confederacy of Dunces,* about life in New Orleans. He was unable to find a publisher after sending out his manuscript many times and it being rejected just as often. In 1969, he killed himself. Whether or not his failure to get published was the core of his depression, we will never know. But we do know that letting other people's opinions determine how we feel about ourselves is dangerous.

Toole's mother, more resilient than her son, refused to give up on publishing the book. She relentlessly sent the manuscript out again and again. It was returned each time, rejected. Eventually, however, she connected with a patron in the form of Walker Percy, a writer. It was Percy who ultimately got the novel accepted by the Louisiana State University Press. In 1980, the book won the Pulitzer Prize for fiction. This shows you that opinions vary widely on good literature and that peoples' tastes are divergent. Walker Percy saw something in Toole's book that the others did not.

Letting yourself become disheartened by others' sentiments can be devastating. What you consider your best idea, someone else may pass off as inconsequential. This does not mean that it is not great. It may indicate, however, that the vision that inspired your thought may not trigger another's imagination. However, if it stimulated you, there are others who will be equally captivated. The trick, then, is to continue the search until you discover those others. Giving up before bringing your project to fruition or becoming defeated because someone sees it differently and has a negative opinion can be destructive. If life teaches us anything, it is that there is always another way to get things done. Mrs. Toole proved that.

Is there a project you deeply care about that requires dedication and a commitment to see through to completion? Is there an idea you believe in, but you are having a hard time recruiting others who agree? If so, use the example of John Kennedy Toole and his mother to remind yourself to stay open to other ways and possibilities of accomplishing the result you desire.

A creativity expert, Roger Von Oech, said it well. "Remember, there are two benefits of failure. First, if you do fail, you learn what doesn't work, and second, the failure gives you an opportunity to try a new approach."

Clearly, what doesn't work is giving up.

Can you imagine a major-league baseball player leading the league in making the most errors, in being struck-out the most times, in hitting into the most double plays, and still being voted Most Valuable Player for that year? It happened in the American League in 1942. Joe Gordon did all those things and still won the MVP award that season.

The lesson here is that, even though you or others have faults, mess up, make mistakes, or operate imperfectly, you can overcome all of this, come back to win again, and be acknowledged for your good deeds. No matter what you have done or what challenges you have experienced, they are but memories in your personal history that cannot, of themselves, create pain for you now unless you keep the pain alive in your awareness.

Often times, because of past training, we are tempted to judge an experience as bad. Once labeled that way, we smugly stuff it in a mental box and securely file it into some unconscious place. Thinking we are cleansed of it, we brush ourselves off and go merrily on our way. Because it was a *bad* experience, we make sure not to let it happen again.

Wrong! Dismissing it too quickly is not smart. Life's challenge is to understand the past so that we discover the principle of cause and effect at work. Also, through careful examination, we can learn to direct our lives in more positive ways, toward desired outcomes.

Think of a time that was particularly challenging: a loss of some sort, bankruptcy, ill-health, divorce, job. Assuming this instance was in the past, how have you changed as a result of this challenge? How are you different, stronger, or wiser than you were before?

Typical answers to these questions include, "I've gotten stronger, more resilient. I appreciate every new day. I've become less judgmental and critical." If the change has seemingly been for the worst, you've become sour, skeptical, more judgmental or angry. In that case, you have not taken advantage of the opportunity to learn valuable lessons.

I have a friend, Rachel, who was losing her eyesight at the same time her long-term job at a large U.S. corporation was downsized and she learned that her husband had gambled away their savings. She was working part-time and about to lose her house when she discovered a business opportunity with a nutritional company that could right everything. She went for it. Within six months, she was able to bring her house payments up to date. Within nine months, she completely regained her eye sight, improved her health, and achieved a stable abundant income.

If Rachel had spent her time in self-criticism and misery and had not been alert and willing to try something new, she would have ended up blind and homeless. The transformation turned out to be radical and positive because she recognized it was time to take a new path in life. Choosing growth over living in the past helps a person experience peace. Sometimes the arrival of difficult circumstances is the only way to wake up. Would Rachel have made any of these changes if her back wasn't against the wall? Would any of us?

To reflect on the past and recognize those times as new beginnings will connect you to your spiritual center. The Universe is always blessing you with new opportunities.

List five challenging situations from the past and identify what each one was to teach you.

Challenging situations of the past:

1.

2.

3.

4.

5.

What have you learned from each of these situations? What can you do now to embrace these lessons? How have they helped you be stronger, better, wiser? How can you use this awareness to be stronger today?

You are living this life to become more than you are and better than you are. People grow from the inside out. Each person is either expanding or decreasing. No one stands still. You get to choose which direction you take.

Self-discipline helps you put aside automatic negative reactions. Generally, these reactions are based on unrealistic expectations and outmoded belief systems. Let's face it, no one has it all together. Nonetheless, consistent self-improvement is a worthy goal.

Successful people often discuss the value of mistakes or failure. Perhaps no one has learned that lesson better than Olympic swimmer Mark Spitz. He said, "The Olympics taught me that, no matter how successful you think you might be, you become actually more successful after you've failed miserably." Spitz's record proves his point. He was the first person to win seven gold medals in a single Olympics year, which took place in 1972. He ultimately won nine gold medals, the most gold medals ever for a swimmer in Olympic history.

Prior to this, in the 1968 Olympics, Spitz lost in two individual events, the 100- and 200-meter butterfly, even though he held world records in both. Following the games, he faced his disappointing performance head-on by carefully analyzing his failure. He realized he had never swum three individual events at the same competition and he had allowed his disappointment at losing one event to carry over into the next. He not only became negative with each loss, his opponent, Doug Russell, got more positive. Thus, Russell went on to win the gold medal.

Mark Spitz spent the next four years preparing for the 1972 Olympics by repairing his mistakes. "You cannot carry what did or did not happen from one day to the next, especially if it is negative, into something that's supposed to be a positive experience for the next day."

He grew mentally and physically strong. He prepared himself to go from event to event, ignoring his prior performance and focusing fully on the next competition. He tried to keep his opponents from gaining too much confidence by beating them soundly in each event. Therefore, in Munich, Germany, the site of the 1972 Olympics, he won seven gold medals and set seven world records.

You can learn the same lessons as Mark Spitz. Don't look back, other than to analyze what happened. Learn from the situation and improve. Keep your attention on the task at hand. Give it 100% effort.

Spitz commented, "Too many people spend too much time keeping score, so it's impossible for them to play the game."

Developing a positive view about problems is often difficult for people to grasp. We often wish to deny imperfections and blame others for our mistakes. Perhaps this lack of realism results from reading fairy tales where everyone lives happily ever after, or from get-rich-quick stories where the starlet is discovered at the soda fountain and moved instantly into fame and fortune, or from the entrepreneur who happens on a great idea and makes millions overnight, or from the first-time novelist who writes a great book and makes the New York Times Bestseller list. Such stories can jade the idea of success, especially if we measure our efforts against them.

There is definitely an attitude necessary to handle short-comings. I have encouraged many perfectionistic people to practice being imperfect. It reduces the pressure immediately and allows a greater sense of freedom. If you accept your inadequacies, you have only one way to go and that is up. Try it! Accept yourself as imperfect and enjoy it. You are a work-in-progress. You have tremendous capabilities and are in the development stage, as is everyone else, whether they know it or not. Mistakes are the gifts that bring this potential into focus.

Speaker Denis E. Waitley said, "Forget about the consequences of failure. Failure is only a temporary change in direction to set you straight for your next success."

Give Praise Instead

Giving self-praise is a most important skill. It makes the difference between living exalted lives and ones that hinge on mediocrity. It must be said that most people have been cautioned that it is bad, perhaps improper, to give yourself credit for accomplishments or abilities. Some even refer to it as bragging. This is a behavioral program with which most of us were raised. But no one told us what happens when you don't honor your talents and skills. When you deprive yourself of positive feedback, the backlash is negative. Results such as low self-esteem, diminished productivity, and lack of motivation become evident.

Since crediting yourself with your natural talents and best efforts is a no-no, people tend to resort to its opposite and more socially acceptable behavior, self-criticism. They find flaws in themselves, lest someone else spot them first. "I could have done better. I am a mess. How stupid of me. My hair is too straight, too curly, too short, too long." You get the idea.

Self-criticism can become a game of one-upmanship. The competition is to be the worst of the worst. I heard a bulimic lady admit, "If I can't be the best, I will be the worst." This was her rationale for eating to excess and then regurgitating. So, who is the winner in this game?

A healthier choice would be to give honest, deserved praise for well-rendered efforts. Accolades spur you on to great achievement. You have many good points. Acknowledge them to yourself. Be honest and clear. You are unique and talented in your own way. Make sure you are supporting yourself and not vying for other's approval.

Judgmental people will consider you egotistical. They are always looking for the negatives. Their fault-finding has no boundaries. If you are talented and resourceful, or unproductive and lazy, they will render equal criticism. Don't let them deter you. Ultimately, it is up to you to decide how important their opinions are and whether or not you wish to agree with them. Once that has been settled and you are determined to listen to your own inner guide of encouragement, you will be able to reap the rewards of a positive self-concept.

Honest praise builds strength, resilience, and self-esteem. These are necessary qualities . As you progress, you will become strong and undefeatable.

Denis Waitley, speaker and author of *The Psychology of Winning*, states that "Praise builds, criticism deteriorates." It is his idea that praise, liberally administered, not only elevates self-esteem, but encourages belief in self. It works like this: as a person starts to like himself, he takes on greater challenges and risks, resulting in productivity increases. Ultimately, even weak, ineffectual attitudes and behaviors are improved. Every aspect of the individual is strengthened.

David Viscott, author of *Risking*, comments, "The more you love yourself, the less dependent you are on others."

People who like themselves are not found on welfare rolls, nor do they linger in depression or lament their troubles to the world. Loving yourself and accepting yourself as productive and possessing positive qualities requires personal and sacred commitment, as well as discipline. It can be controversial, but worth a try.

Here are steps you can take to cultivate a mind-set of self-praise:

- Start by commending yourself for possessing at least five positive attributes. You really have many more. Examples might be patience, perseverance, friendliness, honesty, generosity, kindness.

- Acknowledge good in everything you do. One example might include cleaning the house but forgetting to dust the furniture. Credit yourself for what you did accomplish. If your boss demonstrates a negative mood, credit yourself for remaining pleasant. If you miss a turn on the right street when driving, yet find your way back, give yourself credit for being resilient.

- Give at least five compliments to others daily. This exercise trains your mind to look for positives. It keeps you mentally elevated.

- Look forward with enthusiasm to some scheduled activity daily. Enthusiasm keeps your energy high.

- At the end of each day, give thanks for all the positive occurrences. Don't just look for big triumphs. If you stayed calm when everyone else was ruffled, that is positive. Giving thanks offers extravagant rewards in that you are training yourself to be abundant. The higher your energy, the greater your ability to attract great opportunities.

The switch to self-praise can be inspiring. Fighting the war of low self-esteem requires diligence. This struggle is not won in one battle. The foe of negativity is often deeply entrenched. However, each positive stroke reinforces your value and places you closer to victory.

You possess qualities you can applaud. No one is without virtue or talent. Self-confidence is founded on consistent, honest, and personal praise. Take the risk of becoming a new, exciting you by appreciating your efforts now. Build your value through praise.

How do you do this? When others want to pull you down with criticism, understand that they would have no need for criticism if they were healthy themselves. *Forgive them, for they know not what they do.*

People attack when they feel wounded. By the same token, you indulge in similar behavior. Watch your own critical thoughts and ask yourself, "What is my pain? Can I let it go?" As you discover your own inner wounds, you will be able to forgive yourself and let go. It gets easier.

In time, your positive thoughts will outweigh your negative ones and you will feel good about yourself. It is a process. Enjoy it!

Perfectionism. Drop It!

There is nothing more paralyzing than the idea of perfection. We can never attain it. So, let's be honest about what it means to be our human selves. We are fated to miss the mark of perfection, yet able to achieve small, impressive acts of courage and greatness. Even great heroes have had their flaws. Thomas Jefferson owned slaves, had children with at least one of them, and even allowed them, his own children, to be slaves for a while. Yet, he amassed amazing contributions to society.

Martin Luther King, Jr. had a great vision. He also had extra-marital affairs. John Lennon wrote that "all we need is love," yet he had a difficult relationship with his son.

Forget the idea of being perfect and accept that everyone, including our greatest heroes, are flawed. Period.

Dropping the silly, wasteful belief that you are to be perfect will keep you from setting yourself up for failure and burnout. Instead, move on with the challenges of life, committing to give your best effort day-in and day-out. Be more courageous as you go.

I have known many perfectionists. Their credo is, "If it's worth doing, it's worth doing right." They hate mistakes, anyone's mistakes. Not doing it right, whatever that is, drives them crazy. It becomes a personal affront for them to have to re-do a project or correct *stupid* errors. Of course, this obsession creates tremendous relationship conflicts and pressure because working with or being around a perfectionist is not fun. People who go through life trying to be perfect are beating their heads against a brick wall.

If perfection does exist, it represents limitation. By striving for it, you seek a nebulous state of boundaries. Instead of holding the illusion that there are some flawless people, take inspiration from the fact that our heroes simply brought themselves back on track, probably again and again, whenever their behavior did not match their intent. You can do the same while being courageous enough to quit when it is time

If you were an artist, at what point would you deem your painting or sculpture perfect? Would this decision mean that one more brush stroke, dot, line, or impression would not improve the work?

You can say the same thing about designing a frock, a building, piece of furniture, garden, book, golf game, or anything. There is nothing in the material world that can't be added to or improved.

In their book, *Art and Fear*, David Bayles and Ted Orland tell the story of a ceramics teacher who declared on the opening day of class that he was dividing his students into two groups. One group would be graded on quantity. On the last day of class, he would bring a scale and weigh the pots they had made. With fifty pounds of pots, they would get an A. For 40 pounds, a B etceteras.

The second half of the students would be graded on quality. They just had to produce one perfect pot.

The results were astounding. The group being graded for *quantity* produced all of the works of highest quality. As Bayles and Orland put it, "It seemed that while the quantity group was busily churning out piles of work and learning from their mistakes, the quality group had sat theorizing about perfection and, in the end, had little more to show for their efforts than grandiose theories and a pile of dead clay."

This story indicates that he who is in production, learns the most, and that perfection, as a goal, need go to the bottom of the list.

Of course, there are those who will never be happy with anyone's efforts. These are the ones who busy themselves finding fault. If you were to ask them what perfection is in their instance, they would have a hard time coming up with a reasonable answer. They might say, "I wouldn't run late. The object wouldn't be lopsided. That color would be brighter. People should be this way or behave that way. They should speak a certain way or don't do it."

In other words, they have a lot of rigid ideas of how things should or shouldn't be and an unclear picture of what they seek.

Perhaps they do not calculate the result of striving for the unattainable and the frustration involved. Maybe their real desire is to impress others rather than to learn and grow. Nevertheless, if these perfectionists were to develop a deeper goal, centered on self-improvement, they would increase their sense of fulfillment and self-esteem. Their confidence would grow. They would ultimately release their aggravation and create exponentially greater results.

Perfectionists tend to hold on to a project too long as they believe letting go is a sign of failure. Yet, every venture has an end point. Stopping when it is time to be finished is a sign of genius, not failure. It is similar to selling an investment in company stock when all indications suggest it is time to give it up. If you keep it too long, value is lost. The same is true with everything else.

One can stay in a job or relationship forever, waiting until it is mastered completely. Will that ever happen? What if it doesn't? Have you stayed long enough to accomplish your purpose? When does continuing cost more than it pays? When the positive returns are less than the energy required to remain, it is time to get out or move on. This is true of projects, jobs, relationships, everything.

Does perfectionism exist for you? Have you made it a goal? Be truthful and fair. Honestly assess when enough is enough, when you have given your best, and when it is time to say, "*Adios!*"

You can remain forever where you are and there will always be more to do there. The project will not let you go. You must be the decider. You are the important component. Believe in yourself, give it your best shot, and let go when it is appropriate.

If failure is a lack of perfection, then Tal Ben-Shahar, author of *Choose the Life You Want,* indicates that "You can learn just as much, if not more, from failure as from success."

Walter Russell, in *The Man Who Tapped the Secrets of the Universe,* acknowledged, "I have had my share of what one calls defeat in plenty. I have made and lost fortunes and seen great plans of mine topple through my own errors of judgment or through other causes. . . . But I do not recognize these as defeats. They are but interesting experiences of life. They are valuable stepping-stones to success. Defeat is a condition which one must accept in order to give it reality. I refuse to give it reality by accepting it. In my philosophy, I have written these words: "Defeat I shall not know. It shall not touch me. I will meet it with true thinking. Resisting it will be my strengthening. But if, perchance, they will give to me the bitter cup, it will sweeten in the drinking."

Along those same lines, there aren't any circumstance that couldn't be changed for the better. How? By changing yourself. By accepting yourself for your talents and flaws. Resolve to mine the peace within no matter what the material world appears to reflect.

By plaguing yourself with perfectionist goals, you strive for the unattainable. Frustration is born out of reaching for something that doesn't exist. The seeker, profusely aware of falling short of his goal, develops critical, self-defacing attitudes. This inner critic keeps genius from coming out.

There is something to be said for making mistakes and even failing. Basketball great, Michael Jordan, was cut from his high-school team. His failure to maintain his position on the team created frustration that drove him to persevere and practice, practice, practice. He spent many extra hours on the court developing his prowess. That is how he ultimately developed his genius as a basketball great. He wasn't going for perfection, but performance.

Your perfectionism is your critic and will continually manufacture critical judgments, comments, and opinions. In order to perform, you must still the critic inside. For example, the little boy who wants to learn to ride his bike will jump on it. As he attempts to ride it, he loses his balance and falls off. He tries another way. Eventually, he figures out a way to ride the bike and his performer-self comes out. He wins from his effort.

There is a difference between needing to create perfect results and having high standards. A person with high standards gives his best and learns from the outcome. His aim is to continually improve his skills. Conversely, a perfectionist, expects every effort to be indisputable, without flaw. His ego rides with each outcome and is crushed when criticized.

The perfectionism, the inner critic, is disempowering. Your genius self comes out when you continually improve your performance without worrying about perfection. It could be that what you really want is to do your best. Each time you unconditionally offer your best effort, you add to your ultimate performance, just like Michael Jordan. Give your effort for your own self-gratification and fulfillment, not to impress or please anyone else. Personal acceptance and appreciation is a sign of maturity, an indication that you've given your best.

Seek a healthier perspective. Babies learn to walk over time. We don't expect them to get up once and walk perfectly. We understand that walking is a process that includes various factors, such as balance and strength. Patiently, we applaud each effort the baby makes. With encouragement, babies tenaciously try again and again until they have mastered walking. We are similar.

Each time we venture into new territory or attempt yet another learning experience, we are as fresh and innocent as a baby. Endeavor to express patience and gentleness in your growth process.

Expecting immediate success, without the benefit of trial and error, is unrealistic and unfair. If you mentor others the same way, you insure failure. The results you seek come more quickly by engaging a positive, reinforcing attitude. If your present challenge is to develop a kind, nurturing mindset, allow the necessary time to get there.

Remember life is a process involving continuous adjustments. There are always ways to enhance beauty, balance, and effectiveness. To assume otherwise, discourages on-going engineering, research, and creativity. The automobile industry continues to reengineer in order to improve their products. Technology races onward with newer advanced designs. Why, then, would we assume that a human is not a work-in-progress? There is joy in becoming.

Excellence is an art won by training and habituation.
We do not act rightly because we have virtue or
excellence, but rather we have those because we have
acted rightly. We are what we repeatedly do.
Excellence, then, is not an act but a habit.

—Aristotle, Greek Philosopher

We can often do more for others by trying to correct our
own faults than by trying to correct theirs.

—Francois Fenelon, Catholic Archbishop,
Theologian, and Poet

Chapter Eight

Get Your Ego Out of the Way

In our fear-based world, there are many rules. Most are designed around the idea of survival. Interestingly enough, no one is going to survive. Nevertheless, our instruction is to focus on the future, plan for it, and save for it. There is nothing inherently wrong with putting money aside and not spending every penny you make on sensory gratification, such as cars, costumes, accruements, chocolate. What is wrong is the continual focus on the future that keeps you from being present NOW.

In truth, the future, if there is one, comes out of the present. What you do, think, and act on today will extend into tomorrow. But often, by making the future the goal, we don't invest in the present, in our own current state of affairs, in what we are doing, accepting, and believing right now.

This chapter is called "Get Your Ego Out of the Way" for a reason. It is your egoic self, your personality and sense of separateness from everyone and everything else, that has adopted a set of beliefs that keeps you focused in the past with guilt and remorse. "Why did I do that? Why did I say that?" Focusing on the future, it turns into, "What if this? What if that happens?" More than likely, it will never happen anyway. Either way, you are not present NOW.

Thus, we do our *tribal* planning for the traditional life, one that is safe, comfortable, normal, and not necessarily innovative, expansive, or love-focused. People become entranced with their tribal traditions. The Germans do this, the Italians believe that, the Latinos follow these customs, and the Aborigines follow those. Some dance at funerals, while others are somber. Some groups believe you are to put food out for the dead. Others rotate crops in a particular way, or celebrate when the rain comes. Some might worship a rock. Others believe it is important to sacrifice a goat to insure prosperity. These are tribal customs and beliefs. Man made them up. God did not.

Every person has a dream. Something in the soul, a desire, an image, a hunch, a special interest, that is the key to their heart's desire. Many are afraid to give it credence because it doesn't fit the society norm or expectations of the traditional life, like college, marriage, buying a home, having children, getting a *good* job, having a 401K or pension, retiring, and dying. We laud people who put their children first and deny their own happiness without realizing what consequences that particular model sets up for the kids. Thus, the pattern continues and the tribe expands. The beliefs get stronger.

Along comes someone, a maverick perhaps, who steps out of the tribal circle and says, "I choose to go my own way and follow my dream." He skips college, digs into his personal interest, perhaps starts a business, invents something, becomes an artist or musician, develops a product, innovates in some other way. He begins his soul journey. This is a precarious position because, when he changes from the norm, he is forced to deal with the ego and all its judgments. In other words, the maverick better stay strong, focused, and undeterred if he wants to stay on the path to follow his dream.

Here is how it works for you. Your Inner Guide, which you may see as the Soul, Spirit, the Universe, or God, is not happenstance. You are only given a desire when you also have the inherent talent and ability to fulfill it. In stepping from the tribal group and getting ready to be outrageous, you must be ready to take Spirit as your partner. It is your friend, comfort, and stability. As an innovative maverick, you no longer need to heed *useless* traditional thinking and beliefs that serve no purpose or benefit to anyone. That's right, no more goat sacrifices. You can rotate the crops in whatever way makes sense to you. The independent maverick can give full focus to the urgings of the soul. That is when anything is possible.

The book, *Chicken Soup for the Soul,* written by Jack Canfield and Mark Victor Hanson, was rejected 144 times before a publisher finally read it, loved it, and published it. They did not doubt their vision or determination to get their book published. Their idea was to sell over a million copies by the second year of entering the marketplace. They held no limitation as to its popularity. As it happened, *Chicken Soup for the Soul* was a huge success. It was re-written into 149 variations and sold all over the world. It ultimately became a billion-dollar industry. And yet, they were told "No" many times.

Another incredibly popular book, *Jonathan Livingston Seagull,* by Richard Bach, went through the same process. It was rejected numerous times until finally published to become a New York Times Bestseller for many weeks. Years later, it is still a well-read book about living your dream.

Visionaries create, while the traditional folks, with their eyes on the bottom line, make the decisions. With enough persistence by the visionary, someone *gets* the message, finds value in it, and is willing to invest.

You are continually faced with decisions, large and small. All are important because they set you up for fulfilling your dream and your purpose in life. Think of each decision as another step along your path. The only way you will fulfill your potential is to get your ego and its small beliefs out of the way.

Marissa worked at a corporation for thirty years. This company had been bought and sold several times. With each new management team, the corporate environment got darker, more demanding, and more negative. Because Marissa was a loyal person, took pride in her work, and wanted to stay at the company until she retired, she stayed on, accommodating every change and every idiosyncrasy that came with each new leader. Finally, she broke under the pressure and quit her job.

For over thirty years, Marissa had practically walked on water to get her job done. She had become a human dynamo with accrued skills, talents, resources, and a huge database of associates, all available for her own use. Yet, because she had stayed so long and was so loyal to *them* instead of to herself, she had sacrificed her health and her energy, leaving her spirit depleted.

After a year away from the turmoil, Marissa felt stronger and healthier. She began to retrieve her energy. She started playing around with the idea of developing a logo for a small business. She wanted to help people create ease and beauty in their homes and lives. It was to be a service business providing assistance with gardening, party planning, sprucing up homes, getting organized, and other such things. Her timing was impeccable. The concept had incredible potential.

The problem was that Marissa saw it only as a nice little side business while she envisioned herself as an employee, working in another corporation and continuing to fund her 401K. She had programmed her mind to be at the mercy of employers without realizing she had the skills to be an entrepreneur.

Another problem was that Marissa was smarter, savvier, and more talented than the requirement of the positions she sought. She no longer fit into those jobs. Her tribal beliefs were strong. "You work hard for someone else, put others first, pay off your house, put money away, and someday, you will get to live." In other words, her attention was focused on everyone else and everything other than herself. She definitely was not in the present moment. She was so locked into traditional thinking, she did not even realize that she had a dream: her own business. She did not realize she also had the tools and resources to make it successful.

When I saw her, she was devastated that she had failed at finding a new corporate job. She felt mortified that she had been unable to fund her retirement for a whole year. In her mind, she was a *failure*.

Marissa lived in the future with the *good-girl* mentality, the ego. She had to step out of her grief to see the bigger picture. In her life, she had asked for guidance from God, Jesus, and all things spiritual. Yet, when the guidance came, she could not recognize it because it did not fit her picture. What she was really asking for was guidance to continue in her traditional way. Guess what, God, the Universe does not hold man's traditions sacred. It is not the way Spirit works. You want help? There is help. "That job is not for you. Nor that one. Nor that one."

All was not gloom-and-doom in that there were people waiting to help Marissa. She had to get her pride (ego) out of the way.

She finally woke up to the understanding that God/ Spirit/ Universe had been assisting her all along the way. She had received answers to her prayers. She had created the dream, the resources, and the customer base to manifest a wildly successful business while having a blast doing it. She finally got to work for someone who could and would appreciate her expertise: herself.

The moral of the story is that God has Its own solutions and ways of helping. Don't go to God and declare, "I want this and it has to happen this way and with that person." You just might hear giant peals of laughter rolling through the heavens. The bottom line is that God's way is a better way. Get your ego out of the way. That is how you will do the impossible.

Oprah Winfrey stated, "God had a bigger plan for me than I had for myself."

Well, guess what? God has a bigger plan for you, too.

Louis was unhappy in a loveless marriage for many years. He and his wife Laverne went in separate directions and lived disparate lives. You might even say they didn't like each other, which is a definite sign that a marriage is over.

Louis prayed that his wife would ask him for a divorce. In the meantime, they both got involved with other people.

Finally, Laverne came to Louis and spelled out that she wanted a divorce.

You'll never guess his reaction. Louis was *offended*! In this particular case, what he had asked for was exactly what he got, but instead of gratitude, he was upset. "How could she ask me for a divorce after all I have done for her?"

So there you go! Sometimes you get exactly what you want, and you're still unhappy. Or you receive the guidance you seek so that you can live a life of creativity and abundance, and you're mad that God didn't offer up another limited, miserable experience you thought you wanted. It is all about fear of change. In other words, get your ego out of the way.

In the practice of dissolving or diminishing the ego, you will release all the drama and conflict that goes with it. This will allow you to connect with an energy that is far greater than this small, limited world of form. Of course, the ego will continue to try to convince you that you are nothing more than a form, meaning a body, job, ethnic group, etc., and it is important you prevail in protecting your form identity. This identification as a body, instead of a mind or spirit, sets up continual turmoil and it keeps you small.

To eliminate the ego's mayhem, you must diminish it. You start this by witnessing your reactions. In practicing observation, you will discover numerous events and people that press your buttons. "Why are they behaving that way? I can't understand why she would say such a thing? I think it is terrible what they are doing?" *Blah, blah, blah.* You can keep a log or diary of all the ways you react to people and things. In so doing, you will begin to notice patterns.

When you find yourself in conflict, where something has not gone your way, where someone is mad at you, or you are angry, you find yourself in victim-mode. You want to blame, accuse, defend, justify, gossip, make yourself right, make someone else wrong, complain, make judgments, or be offended, STOP! Become alert. Don't do anything. That is to say, instead of following the ego's script and entering into the drama, STOP! Decide not to participate.

Every time you become non-reactive and choose not to partake in arguing, offensive behavior, ego-drama, or who is right and who is wrong, you let go of chaos, attachment, and smallness. You embrace freedom and peace. Each time you step aside, you free energy.

You might ask, "But what if that person is wrong?"

The answer is, "What if they are?"

Allowing others to have their delusions is part of the game. You can pretend you are right, if you wish. Yet, the more you let go of all of that, the freer you will feel.

Let's go back to the example of driving your car in heavy traffic. You are intent on getting to your destination on time when some crazy person rushes past you and almost sideswipes your car. He cuts in front of you, almost colliding with your car, then continues driving erratically down the road. Do you shake your fist and rail at the person? Do you catch up with him in traffic and give him a piece of your mind? Or do your let go and remain in peace? You can see the consequences of each action.

The question is, "Are you dedicated to having peace and living from a Higher Authority?" The more you let the world have its drama and you choose peace, the more you have diminished your ego-self and replaced it with the greater energy of peace. That makes mental space for you to be guided to a wonderful new reality. This practice of letting go is a powerful spiritual practice.

When you are altering your normal reactions, you may feel uncomfortable for a few seconds, as though you have shrunk in size. Then, you may sense an inner spaciousness that feels vast and alive. You have not diminished, but your ego has. You have actually expanded.

I had a student who realized she was hung up on being right and not being wrong. I told her that her assignment was to be wrong everyday in some capacity and discover what happens. She agreed to do this.

The next day, her opportunity came in the form of a parent-teacher conference. When the teacher corrected her regarding her child's behavior, she stopped and did not defend herself. It was uncomfortable, as she was not used to this new way of being. She was letting go of her ego's need to be right. And she did it. Soon, she was laughing to herself because she realized that being right meant nothing and being wrong took nothing from her. She did not feel diminished at all. She felt exalted.

Here is the amazing realization: when it appears you are diminished in some way, and continue to remain non-reactive, externally and internally, you understand that nothing real has been lost. By becoming less, you actually become more. When you choose not to defend or attempt to strengthen the mental form you have created of yourself, you step out of identification with form and self-image. Who you are becomes *real,* and the need to defend yourself is gone. You are free! You are literally transformed. The energy that was trapped in maintaining your self-image is released for greater expression. You begin to radiate a greater self. This is what leads you to doing the impossible.

Be clear. This is not about inviting abuse or becoming a rug for others to wipe their feet. Those situations can be handled with reason and right action. This exercise is about dissolving unnecessary egoic reactions and wasting energy to preserve a false self.

Here is an exercise.

When someone criticizes you, blames you, or calls you names, instead of retaliating or defending yourself, do nothing. Refusing to be drawn into the other's drama separates you from the ego's concoction of who you are. It moves you into vastness and freedom.

In time, when someone tries to manipulate you or elicit a response that is not in your best interest, you will laugh because the whole maneuver will seem nonsensical and ridiculous.

Where Does *Fitting In* Fit In?

Once, a fellow asked me a question, stated as follows. "I am a successful entrepreneur and find I have a problem fitting in with normal society. I attend lots of meetings and social functions. I am continuously disappointed to find that I operate on a different wavelength than other people. I seek connection, friendship, and sharing. Instead, I find a lot of fear-based naysayers with whom I don't relate. How can I find people I can enjoy?"

I said, "Perhaps you are looking for companionship in the wrong places. It sounds like the naysayers you describe as *normal* relive past events, or complain about things without seeking solutions, or reside in comfort zones where new ideas are not explored. Many folks avoid the excitement of change or new learning opportunities, maybe even feeling put off by them.

"But that is okay, because when you let go of the people who don't fit in your world, you open to those who do. Accepting the idea that you don't have to *fit in* with everybody, frees you to seek other more positive, rewarding interactions."

As a successful business owner, perhaps you are a doer, optimistic, goal-oriented, and risk-taking, someone who thinks more about what can be accomplished in a given situation than what is eternally wrong with it. In that way, your mode of perceiving the world doesn't fit with fear-based negative people. Thus, do you lament this fact or give thanks?

The good news is that there are people who operate on a more positive, elevated wave-length. These are the doers, the movers and shakers. For them, living in a society of victims is unacceptable and maybe even ridiculous. Your job is to locate these big-picture folks.

So, where are they?

Look for groups where growth is a major topic. It could be business organizations, entrepreneurs, Toastmasters, personal or business growth classes, or even golf clubs. Open your mind to all kinds of possibilities. And most of all, value the truth that you were never meant to be ordinary. It will free you to discover interesting, satisfying connections with other achievers.

Thomas Edison associated with Henry Ford. Wouldn't you have loved to listen to their conversations? Billionaires like Bill Gates and Warren Buffett hang out together.

None of the greatest leaders, inventors, technicians, engineers, teachers, and artists were *normal* as the world would perceive normal. These people seem far from normal in their daily lives. In fact, each was abnormal or supernormal. They marched to a different drummer. They did not follow a cultural script. They operated *out of the box*. They were tuned to a different voice, perhaps the still small voice inside that has no limits. Because of this, they accomplished miraculous things. The world might say they weren't qualified. Most corporations would not even hire them because they did not fit into the rigid criteria or cultural norms.

These were the non-conformists, like Orville and Wilbur Wright, who didn't buy into the idea that man was never meant to fly, like Thomas Edison, who allowed you to flick a switch and light your home with electricity, like Alexander Graham Bell, who made it possible for you to talk to someone across the nation or world. These were the kinds of people, like Bill Gates, who believed there could be a computer in every home, and like Henry Ford, who made travel by motor vehicle available to everyone.

These misfits catered to a bigger, higher vision of impossible accomplishments. They said *yes* when others said *no* to their imaginations. They believed that if they had an idea, it must be achievable. They did not let poverty, abuse, or the lack of proper nutrition or education get in their way. All that was irrelevant and inconsequential. In fact, these deprivations often spurred them on and fueled them with inspiration and motivation. Some might say it provided an edge or advantage.

Fitting in with others' worlds is a way to be ordinary. Successful people are anything but ordinary. Disdain this fact. Or celebrate it!

Here is a clue called the Carnegie Secret by Napoleon Hill: *All achievement, all earned riches, have their beginning in an idea! If you are ready for the secret, you already possess one half of it; therefore you will readily recognize the other half the moment it reaches your mind.*

What is your wildest, most outrageous idea? Who do you need to talk to? What do you need to do to investigate it further?

Take Risks to Grow

The willingness and ability to take risks to achieve your end goal or to live your values is an important quality. Actually, you cannot become outrageous and do the impossible without taking risks.

Many people think you have to be *brave* to take risks. This is only partly true. The other side of risking involves seeing your reward.

Gutsy people don't risk for the fun of it but, rather, to achieve an objective. I am not talking about recklessness, like jumping off cliffs, driving your car too fast, or investing your life's savings in a questionable stock. I am referring to more basic experiences, such as interrupting a long, boring conversation, stating an unpopular opinion, being alone, introducing yourself to a stranger, or asserting yourself when you feel misused. These risks, which you are faced with daily, make up the fiber of your life and speak of your commitment to grow in self-acceptance and love.

Each time you chance expressing yourself openly, you face the possibility of another's' rejection. However, you also face the prospect of greater self-respect. Respect leads to self-acceptance, which results in motivation. Who do you want to be? What do you want to accomplish? Examine the risks necessary to reach those goals. What is it going to take?

Recently, a man named John came to see me. He felt stuck in his job. It appeared his job review did not accurately reflect his eagerness, determination, and commitment to do good work. Upon reflection, he realized that he was most alive when he was given a project and allowed the freedom to do it without being micro-managed. Our discussion revealed that he liked being in charge with broad parameters to accomplish his task. As he described his career needs, it became apparent that his answer was to be self-employed. Furthermore, John had a vision of what he loved doing and knew he had the skills to accomplish it. So, what was the problem?

The problem was *risk*. Some think that going on their own means they have no safety net. If they fall, there will be no one to catch them, and they will surely crash and burn. The trouble with this idea is that the opposite is also true. In a corporate setting, they are also on their own. They must still trust their ability and continually grow their skills. Unfortunately, there is dependency on others' appraisal of their performance and the risk of being downsized.

Ultimately, there is risk in staying in an unhappy job situation, and there is risk in moving on. Which risk is bigger? Which one is worth taking? It's an individual decision.

In John's case, staying at his job looked like keeping himself small and squashed. Thus, he chose to explore the requirements of creating a career that would provide rewards and a positive environment. He put together a plan to create his own consulting firm. He decided to use all the experience he had accrued in the corporate world to set up and negotiate contacts and act as an emissary for other contractors. This is called a *garage business* because it starts on a small scale and grows from *garage-size* to whatever the person wants it to be.

John started at the point where he was. He assessed his expertise and acknowledged a treasure-trove of value he could bring to others. In fact, crediting himself was the first risk he faced. Next, he assembled a plan on how to bring this expertise to those needing his services. Of course, the plan would change over time. The thing that wouldn't change was John's belief in himself and his willingness to act on it.

John recognized that the only way he could be who he really wanted to be was to express more boldly, to brazenly share his thoughts, ideas, and opinions. As he proceeded along those lines, not only did his career change, but his relationships improved. John discovered that by being himself, he had a lot to offer and was happy.

In the Bible story, Moses took a chance when he left Egypt for the Promised Land. Not only was he responsible for his own safety, but for the Israelites as well. Moses could have let his fear of the unknown territory stop him, but he didn't. He trusted his guidance and the group eventually arrived at their destination in the Promised Land. It took forty years. Moses did not let shortages, enemy attacks, or internal unrest interfere. He kept progressing.

You don't have to cross the Red Sea to stretch yourself. However, viewing your goal as *your* Promised Land will motivate you.

Courage is a matter of conviction. You have conviction about things that are important to you, like nutrition, an exercise routine, a personal style, religious and political positions, and your value systems. Decide how important your goal is to you. If it's a high priority, there will be a burning desire and strong determination to accomplish it. If it is not a strong desire, what can you do to make it so? What do you need to do to develop belief in yourself? What are the steps you must take?

Study successful people to find these answers. Use them as models and listen with your heart for the rest of what you need to know.

Risking is hard when you don't see a benefit. Therefore, take risks that help you move to a clear objective. In time, fear dissipates and is replaced with excitement. Self-respect expands as you walk through your personal desert and you will ultimately arrive at your Promised Land. It probably won't take forty years either. Just keep walking!

In 1519, Herman Cortés, with 600 Spaniards, sixteen or so horses and eleven boats, landed on a vast inland plateau, the Yucatan Peninsula. The Spanish conquistador and his men were about to embark on an adventure to conquer an empire that hoarded some of the world's greatest treasure, including gold, silver, and precious Aztec jewels. However, the odds of overcoming such vast territories with his small army were not good. So, he decided on a dramatic strategy.

Cortés, being well aware that no army had been able to colonize these lands for hundreds of years, took an outrageous approach. Instead of charging through cities and forcing immediate battle, he remained on the beach and awakened the souls of his men with emblazoned speeches. He stirred their spirit of adventure and thirst for fortune. What was meant to be a military exploit became, instead, an extravagant romance in the imaginations of Cortés' troops.

Despite all this, it was the uttering of only three words that altered the history of the New World. As the troops marched inland to face their enemies, Cortés ordered, "**Burn the boats**." This brazen order meant there would be no exit-route.

Remarkably, the command to burn the boats meant that his men had but two choices: die or win victory. And fight they did. His risk to burn the boats panned out successfully because Cortés became the first man in over 600 years to successfully conquer Mexico.

More currently, famed quarterback Peyton Manning found himself without a team when the Indianapolis Colts released him after fourteen seasons. For the first time in his career, Manning had to find a team, and it was a tough choice. He auditioned for the Arizona Cardinals, the San Francisco 49ers, and others before deciding to sign with the Denver Broncos. Manning was clear about his choice.

He said, "It was a hard decision. I had to pick one team and I wanted to go to all of them. But, like the other decisions I made in my life, I decided to make it and not look back. To go from now and make it the right decision. I have to go to work to make it the right decision."

Manning took a risk and made a hard choice. Throughout the process, he never considered his fate because it was outside his control. His focus was on hard work. He knew that to be a success with his new team and make sure his decision was a good one, it was up to him to commit to hard work. This decision gave Manning an edge to create the outcome he wanted. If he failed, it would be despite his greatest efforts. That is the true definition of risk-taking. You do it with the end goal in mind and you remain focused.

The word *decide* comes from the Latin *de cire*, which means *to cut*. Cortes and Manning cut off other options and hustled to make their choices work.

Fortunately, none of us will have to take risks of such magnitude as conquering a country or walking through the desert to save a nation. Yet, when your back is up against the wall, making a bold move is a shrewd strategy.

Thomas Carlyle said, "The courage we desire and prize is not the courage to die decently, but to live manfully."

Norman F. Dixon stated, "The best measure of courage is the fear that is overcome."

Samuel Johnson indicated that "Whatever enlarges hope will exalt courage."

Beverly Smith proclaimed the concept in simple terms. "To be courageous means to be afraid, but to go a little step forward anyway."

Are you courageous enough to take the necessary risks that will move you toward your goal?

You were born with wings,
why prefer to crawl through life?
—Jalaluddin Rumi, Persian Poet and Sufi Mystic

In matters of principle, stand like a rock.
In matters of taste, swim with the current.
—Thomas Jefferson, American Founding Father

It's not what you say, it's what you do;
don't pay attention to how old you are,
only focus on how old you feel.
—Sister Madonna Buder, The Iron Nun

■

Chapter Nine

What Does It Take to Unleash Your Power?'

Characteristics of Success

Even though everyone has it inside of them, not everyone is willing to unleash their inner power of motivation, creativity, and determination. This chapter is about what it takes to get excited and bring up your power so that you can be the outrageous person that does the impossible as easily as ordering your morning latté. But first, a little story from an artist friend of mine.

Lance is a budding and talented artist who has fun showing his work at a weekly Swap Meet in Arizona. Lots of people walk up to him and comment, "I always wished I could paint like that."

"Have you ever tried?" he responds.

They shake their heads and say, "Oh, no, I could never do anything like that."

Lance, who himself had taken up painting relatively recently, exclaims, "How can you know if you don't try? I never thought I could do it either, but one day, I wanted to see if I could. Now look at what I have accomplished."

The people slowly back away, affirming within themselves that it could never happen for them. They are denying their own creative powers. And you know what? It won't happen for them per their own decree.

You get the point. There are qualities and characteristics that separate the folks who are willing to be outrageous and do the impossible from those who won't. Seeing life as an adventure and a place to learn, definitely sets you on a path of discovery.

In this chapter, I will list some of the important attributes that it takes to generate the fire inside to move through obstacles. I will include examples of real-life, inspiring stories that will show you how other people used these attributes to achieve their goals.

Persistence: Flap those Butterfly Wings

Botanist Alfred Russell Wallace, a contemporary of Charles Darwin, conducted a laboratory experiment involving an emperor butterfly. The butterfly was fighting and struggling to get free from its cocoon. Wallace decided to assist the process so he cut a slit the length of the cocoon to help the butterfly exit. The butterfly emerged from the cocoon, spread its wings, drooped perceptibly, and died.

Wallace concluded that, because the butterfly had been denied the struggle out of the cocoon, it had failed to grow. It entered the world lacking the necessary strength to survive.

The same thing happens when we over-protect our children, families, or friends. When we help them avoid responsibility for their actions, we disable them. We also do not develop when we avoid meeting our obstacles head on. In that moment, we may feel that we are helping them or ourselves, but that is far from true.

To be outrageously successful, you have to build a specific set of muscles that allow you to face your challenges squarely. In so doing, you develop the vision, stamina, determination, and self-trust necessary to navigate beyond the task into new, expanded territory. To deny a person the opportunity to grow, take risks, and learn how to accomplish is a dire mistake.

The Iron Nun, Sister Madonna Buder, is a study in persistence. Born in Saint Louis, Missouri, in July 1930, she never was into running as a child, but she was clearly born with a determined streak. She entered the convent in her early twenties and though active, didn't become a committed athlete until hearing the urgings of a Catholic priest during a retreat on the Oregon Coast. Here is her story.

After twenty-six years as a nun in various orders, Sister Madonna joined with thirty-eight other Sisters from varying backgrounds to establish a new, non-traditional community called the Sisters for Christian Community. Independence from the authority of the Roman Catholic Church allowed Buder the freedom to choose her own ministry and lifestyle. It was at this point that she found her second calling, running.

Because there were no organized races, including marathons and triathlons for women, Sister Madonna, at forty-eight, started running for fun. "Father John told me it would be good for my body and mind."

It wasn't until 1977 that she ran her first race. She wasn't sure if it was okay to be running races, since she was the only nun doing so. She wanted to run for charity, but the public might not be ready for a nun running. She was not sure how the media would handle it, either. Thus, to avoid scandal, she checked it out with the bishop. She asked for his blessing.

The bishop replied, "Sister, I wish some of my priests would do what you are doing."

With the deal sealed, Sister Madonna ran her first 8.2-mile race *backwards* because the only place she had trained was on a tennis court. After that, she joined a running group and eventually learned of the Ironman Triathlon.

The steely nun competed in her first triathlon in Banbridge, Ireland, at age fifty-two. The course was hilly. She swam in the "darn cold water" before wetsuits were invented and rode a second-hand men's bike she had secured from a police auction. She finished the race feeling good. "I felt an immense amount of accomplishment after I finished that race. I was content."

After completing the 2005 Hawaii Ironman at seventy-five-years of age, she earned the title, "The Iron Nun." She completed the race one hour before the seventeen-hour midnight cutoff time. She also attained the record for the oldest woman ever to finish the race. The following year, she beat her own record.

She eventually became the overall Ironman world-record holder for finishing the Subaru Ironman Canada in August 2012. This is when the public started to know her name.

Sister Madonna Buder is now eighty-five years old, has run more than 340 triathlons, including forty-five full Ironmen, and doesn't know what all the fuss is about. In her book, *The Grace to Race*, she shares the no-nonsense spirit and deep faith that inspired her extraordinary journey to championship finish lines all over the world. She holds dozens of records, has broken dozens of bones, and speaks of dozens of miracles and angels that propelled her along the way.

"It is my faith that has carried me through life's ups and downs. Whenever injured, I wait for the Lord to pick me up again and set me on my feet, confidently reminding Him, 'God you know, my intent is to keep running toward you.'" Sister Madonna's words of faith regarding her ups and downs define her inner conviction and stamina.

Strength is accrued by facing problems, learning from mistakes, and starting over again. Experience is our great teacher. As with all great achievers, and as illustrated by the butterfly, the pain and intensity of the struggle creates the personal stamina that translates into waking the passion within, which then has the intensity to manifest the impossible.

Although, we don't tend to welcome adversity, pain, or struggle with a positive approach, we can maintain perspective and recognize them as the way to expand and excel in life. With a positive mindset, we not only defeat adversity, but build the skills necessary to do the impossible.

Another icon, Oprah Winfrey, persevered through dire circumstances to succeed in becoming world renowned and one of the richest women in show business. After experiencing a childhood of abuse, poverty, incest, rape, weight-issues, and insecurities, she became famous as the host of the Oprah Show, which aired on television for twenty-five years. Additionally, she created *O Magazine*, held personal growth seminars all over the country, and started her own cable television network.

Winfrey became resilient and strong by transcending her personal difficulties. She is living proof that overcoming hardship supplies resolve, wisdom, and, in her case, fortune.

Winfrey has done the impossible and taught millions of others that they can, too. Her charitable endeavors are as epic as her show business accomplishments. She has given away millions of dollars to help educate others. She even started a school for girls in Africa, which she continues to fund. Oprah, as she is called, is a living example of the power of persistence.

Courage : You Can make a Difference

Merriam-Webster Dictionary defines courage as strength of mind to carry on in spite of danger. Following are stories of amazing people who carried on despite injury and hazard. Each, in their own way, perceived a bigger picture of what was needed and took the reins, despite adversity, pain, and threat, to accomplish a higher purpose. Each demonstrated the true meaning of courage.

Harriet Tubman is the definition of courage. Born into slavery, she was literally and figuratively scarred for life when she refused to aid in the abuse of another slave on the Maryland plantation where she grew up. The overseer, in his rage, threw a heavy iron weight and inadvertently hit Harriet in the head, leaving her with a deep scar and days of unconsciousness. Throughout her life, she suffered from this injury, which set the tone for her achievements. It was this kind of abuse that set her on her mission.

A fearless visionary, Harriet Tubman led scores of her fellow slaves to freedom as a conductor on the Underground Railway. She also went into enemy camps to spy during the Civil War. In so doing, she supplied useful information that helped the Union Army win the war.

Her story starts in 1849 while still a young woman. She set off on a dangerous journey to self-liberation. Fearful that she and the other slaves were going to be sold, she ran away with her two brothers. The brothers turned back, but she pushed onward, following the North Star until she reached Philadelphia. There, she obtained work as a household servant and saved her money so she could return to help other slaves escape.

In the 1850's, Tubman returned to Maryland numerous times in successful, secretive missions to rescue many others. Driven by her love of family, freedom, community, and faith, she dedicated herself to fighting for liberty and equality for the remainder of her long life. Her fearless escapades in the Underground Railway earned her the biblical name, Moses. She struggled against amazing odds and never wavered from her commitment to liberation and civil rights. As a spy, she battled courageously behind enemy lines during the Civil War. It was her mission to bring information to the Union Army so that they could defeat the Confederacy. In her twilight years, after the war and in spite of racist politicians, she worked tirelessly for Civil Rights.

Harriet Tubman did the impossible by carrying out incredibly risky rescues with practically no resources. She stayed true to her cause despite personal pain and suffering. Tubman was a true American hero and an inspiration for all who value freedom.

Speaking of courage, none would exemplify it better than Irena Sendler, another amazing humanitarian. Like Harriet Tubman, Sendler is an astonishing example of putting her own safety aside to meet a greater need. She took incredible risks, saving many people in the process.

Her story takes place in a Polish ghetto under Nazi supervision during World War II. She had received permission to work in the Warsaw ghetto as a plumbing/sewer specialist, and she held an ulterior motive. As she entered the ghetto, she carried a toolbox. When she left, she smuggled a Jewish infant out in the bottom of her toolbox. Additionally, she carried a burlap sack in the back of her truck for larger kids. She kept a dog in the back of the truck. She had trained the dog to bark when Nazi soldiers let her in and out of the ghetto. The soldiers wanted nothing to do with the dog and its barking, which covered the noises made by the kids and infants.

Sendler put her life in jeopardy, over and over, as she ventured into the ghetto to save these babies and children. She managed to smuggle out 2500 kids and infants before getting caught. When the Nazis captured her, they were severe in their treatment. They broke both her legs and arms and beat her severely. But she survived.

Sendler kept a record of the names of all the kids she had smuggled out in a glass jar, which she had buried under a tree in her backyard. After the war, she tried to locate parents who may have survived. She attempted to reunite the families. Most of the parents had died in gas chambers, and the kids she had saved were placed into foster families, homes, or adopted. Irena Sandler's remarkable story demonstrates the actions of a true hero. She died in 2008 in Warsaw, Poland, at ninety-eight years of age.

There are many courageous people who stand out in the time of war. I couldn't resist including another story of a Polish hero, Witold Pilecki. He may be the only person to purposefully get himself incarcerated in Auschwitz during World War II. As a resistance fighter in conquered Poland, Pilecki set out to be arrested and sent to Auschwitz.

During this war, millions of Jewish people and other perceived enemies of the Nazis were sent to their death in concentration camps. Upon hearing of the massive atrocities being done in the camps, thirty-year-old Witold Pilecki volunteered to enter Auschwitz and secretly collect intelligence to be passed on to the resistance and the Allies. He wanted to document and gather evidence to convince the outside world what the Germans were doing. He was interred there for two to three years, after which he escaped.

Pilecki transmitted information about the staggering number of deaths at the camp by smuggling dispatches to the resistance in the laundry. His messages played a huge part in helping the Allies understand the urgency of their liberation movement.

Pilecki escaped in 1943 by overpowering a night guard. He did this with assistance from two Polish comrades.

Lieutenant John Cagno gives us a more current example of courage and heroism. He is a decorated fire-fighter in North Providence, Rhode Island. He grew up as a troubled child without a father. At sixteen, he began volunteering as a firefighter. For Cagno, that was akin to finding the missing piece of the puzzle to his life. He felt he could finally do something worthwhile. He became a professional firefighter.

One day, while climbing a ladder to the third floor of a burning building, he got too close to high-tension transmission wires and his body was jolted with 14,000 volts of electricity. He was burned badly over his entire body and in unbearable pain. He prayed every night that God would take him.

One night, he saw a television show that featured a female gymnast who had one arm amputated below the elbow. She performed amazing feats on the uneven parallel bars. Though she had been injured and dealt with difficult problems, she had found the courage to go on. As a result, she accomplish incredible stunts and enjoyed her life.

Seeing that woman created a turning point for Cagno. He was inspired to make it through his painful recovery. "I looked at her and I realized that she made a tremendous handicap into nothing more than an inconvenience. So I mirrored her actions. I decided to look at my injuries as a little inconvenience. The inspiration I found in her helped me know that, no matter what my outcome, I'd be okay. It gave me the strength I needed to keep fighting."

One day, the fire chief told him, "This won't make sense to you now, but things happen for a reason. Something is going to come out of this, because you didn't die. You have a purpose, and eventually, you'll know what that purpose is."

Cagno says that the purpose was to use his experiences in a positive way, so he could give hope, strength, and understanding to others. He has a much greater empathy for people who are struggling to find the courage they need to overcome the stumbling blocks of life.

Courage doesn't necessarily involve risking your life. Every time you choose to enter unknown territory, you are being courageous. That could be stepping away from the easy way to conquer difficult tasks, leaving tribal beliefs to follow your heart, taking on a challenge that seems bigger than you. These are all acts of valor.

Every person has courage. It is brought forth in various ways. What value do you hold so high that you would risk your well-being to safeguard it?

Optimism: Where Is that Darn Island When You Need It?

Dr. Susan Vaughn, author of _Half Empty, Half Full: Understanding the Psychological Roots of Optimism,_ describes an experiment involving rats. The rats were divided into two groups and placed in tanks of water where they were made to swim for a period of time. The first group had a small island under the water where they could periodically rest their feet. The second group lacked this advantage and, in order to survive, had to continuously swim like crazy. At the end of the time period, both groups were removed from the water, dried, and rested.

Phase two of the experiment involved each rat singularly swimming in a vat without an island or place to rest. The results proved significant in that the first group of rats, those that previously had been able to occasionally rest, swam twice as long as the second group, who had not been able to rest. The presumption was that, having remembered the island, the first group expected to find it, which would allow them to rest. The *island* memory supposedly inspired the group to swim harder and longer. Consequently, the optimistic rats persevered.

Okay, we are not rats, but the conclusion still holds. There is an advantage to being optimistic. Dr. Vaughan makes the point that everyone can become an optimist. It is not so much a tendency or personal disposition, but an active internal process of illusion-building not unlike learning to fly. Vaughn's further deduction is that *reality is overrated*. I couldn't have said it better myself.

Reality refers to *present conditions*. However, conditions are always changing. With optimism, the potential for change includes positive possibilities. With pessimism, that is not the case. In truth, we are always creating our reality, positive or negative. We are the architects of our lives.

Psychiatrist Viktor Frankl, author of *Man's Search for Meaning* and a survivor of the Nazi death camps, including Auschwitz, agrees. Frankl states that, "We cannot avoid suffering, but we can choose how to cope with it, find meaning in it, and move forward with renewed purpose." Frankl held that, "Our primary drive in life is not pleasure, but the discovery and pursuit of what we personally find meaningful." We ultimately construct our own meanings.

Thus, optimism is about how you interpret or give meaning to your experience. Optimists view themselves as vital and in control of their lives. If that is an illusion, it works to their benefit. People notice and respond favorably to optimists. That, by itself, supplies huge advantages in career, love, relationships, and all areas of life. Health, popularity, and success are improved with a positive perspective.

A Harvard study cites that "High amounts of optimism at age twenty predicted good health at sixty-five." As with the rats, optimism provides a welcome island of relief that makes life less frantic and more manageable.

General Colin Powell is reported to have the following edict in his office: *Perpetual optimism is a force multiplier.*

Bottom line: Expecting to find what you want often leads to a self-fulfilling prophecy of success.

Enthusiasm: Fire Up Some Emotion and Show Me What You've Got!

Enthusiasm is one of the most important components of living an outrageously successful life. Frank Bettger, a former second-baseman for the Saint Louis Cardinals, made that point in his book. He tells about playing for a minor-league team in Pennsylvania where the manager told him, "Frank, I don't like firing you because you're a good baseball player, but you haven't got any enthusiasm to play baseball. So, I've got to let you go."

Bettger then played for a Delaware team in an even lower league with the same unenthusiastic attitude.

One day, one of the players asked him, "Frank, don't you like to play baseball?"

"Oh, yes, I love it," he responded.

"Then play it like you love it. You've got to be enthusiastic. Go out there and act enthusiastic."

"But, I don't feel enthusiastic," answered Frank.

"Act as though you do and you'll get it."

Bettger's next stop was with a New Haven team. The first day, the temperature on the field soared to ninety degrees in the shade, but Frank ran the bases like a man electrified. He threw the ball with such force that it seared the hands of the other players. He acted like a man let loose. He swung at every ball, good ones, bad ones, all of them, resulting in several good hits.

The following day, the New Haven newspaper asked, "Where did our team get this human dynamo? This man is super enthusiastic." They named him Pep Bettger.

Before long a scout for the Saint Louis Cardinals visited and hired him. Thus, in one season, he moved up from a Class-D team to the National League where he completed a distinguished career.

Frank Bettger always had the ability to play baseball. When he added enthusiasm to the mix, he became dynamic, one of the greatest second-basemen of all time. His said, "What is the use of living if you don't give it all you've got?"

Richard Turere also models enthusiasm. He used his enthusiasm for invention to engineer a smart solution that would overcome a major problem in his Kenyan village. Like most thirteen-year-old boys in Kenya, Turere was responsible for safeguarding his family's livestock. "We are enemies," he said about the large cat predators who come out of the nearby Nairobi National Park to prey on cows, goats, and sheep.

The villagers' traditional solution to fend off the raiding lions had always been to stab or poison them. But Turere observed something that made it possible to stop killing the African lions. He noticed that the only time the lions did not perform their nocturnal livestock raids was when someone was walking around with a flashlight. The lions were afraid of people and probably equated the torch light with humans. His sharp observation led to his invention of "Lion Lights," to his subsequent status as a villager, and indeed, to one of the world's wildlife heroes.

Turere used LED bulbs from broken flashlights and wired them to a box with switches. He rigged an automated lighting system, powered from solar panels and an old car battery the family used to operate their TV. He attached the "Lion Lights" to poles around the livestock enclosure, and set them to flash in sequence, giving the impression that someone was walking around the enclosure with a torch.

It turned out that Turere's invention became an elegant way to protect his family's cattle from lion attacks. It kept the lions away. Neighbors started asking for similar set-ups to protect their livestock. And the Kenyan government, which paid millions of shillings to communities for livestock loss, was supportive of this hero's invention because it stopped the lion predators one-hundred-percent.

Richard Turere's story was discovered during a worldwide talent search last year in Kenya. He currently attends Brookhouse School, where he won a scholarship as a result of his invention. Turere is an amazing example of what a kid with enthusiasm and creativity can do to solve problems and achieve great things.

"One year ago," he said, "I was just a boy in the savanna grassland herding my father's cow. I used to see planes flying over, and I told myself that, one day, I'll be there inside. And here I am today. I got a chance to come by plane for my first time for my TED presentation."

He hasn't seen anything yet, as his journey is just getting started. If he can solve one of his nation's problems at thirteen years of age, imagine what Turere's will do as he matures.

Are you giving it all you've got? Where do you need to add enthusiasm?

Authenticity: Kick Off Your Shoes and Let's Chat

Authenticity can be a matter of simplicity. When one is truly comfortable with oneself, the trappings of success can seem frivolous and unimportant. Will Rogers experienced great success from his newspaper columns and stage, radio, and movie appearances. His celebrity status garnered him all the money he would ever need. Yet, he never lost his signature simplicity. He continued to wear his rumpled general-store-style clothing and enjoyed a Spartan-type comfort from his minimalist furnishings. At the height of his popularity, the furniture in his dressing room reflected who he was. It consisted of two old straight-backed wooden chairs.

Rogers' wife Betty wanted to surprise him by redecorating his dressing room and providing a bit more comfort. She purchased two soft, comfortable armchairs, a chaise lounge, drapes, lamps, and an Oriental rug, everything a celebrity of his caliber might enjoy. Rogers seemed sincerely appreciative of her thoughtfulness.

Days later, she returned to the dressing room thinking he might be relaxing in one of his new comfortable chairs. Instead, she found him sitting on the floor cross-legged. He commented that he couldn't find any place to sit that suited him. Betty understood. Within a few days, Rogers' dressing room was restored to its original state. His simple, functional chairs came back, for they were what matched his character. He was not ostentatious, and neither were they.

Will Rogers was always authentic and unpretentious, and he became influential because of it. He stated it best when he said,

"I use only one set method in my little gags and that is to try and keep to the truth." Indeed, he was a master of simple truth.

Layne Walker is another example of a fellow committed to being his authentic self. Growing up, he did not do well in school. This is not unusual for outrageous people, because they generally learn in ways different from the norm.

Walker dropped out of high school in his senior year and, over the next thirteen years, held many jobs, some lasting a few days, others a few months, none as long as a year. Restless and dissatisfied, he could find nothing that fit. Finally, his step-dad introduced him to installing ceramic tile. In the process, he discovered that doing things on his own, rather than being told how to do them, was the way he liked to learn. He started his own tile-setting business, which lasted twenty-five years.

In the meantime, Walker loved to read novels. While setting tile one day, he met an author who was writing a book. Writing sounded like fun to him, so he decided to write a book, too. He made it through two pages before he quit in frustration. "Who am I kidding? I didn't complete high school, let alone attend college, so how can I expect to write a book?" He also tried art. "The horse I drew looked like a cross between a giraffe, an elephant, and a dog." (Sounds a little like Picasso to me.)

Years later, he met his soul-mate Anne, who happened to be an editor, critiquing novels for a living. Reading some of the manuscripts she was editing, Walker pointed to one and said, "This story is terrible." Thinking he could do better, he decided to try writing again, this time with guidance.

He immediately taught himself how to type. He joined a writer's group and, one year later, self-published his first book, a short-story collection. Two months later, he published an action-adventure novel. "Wow," he said, "now I am an author. I went from a high-school dropout to a published author." He has since published three more novels and is working on more.

Two women in his writer's group asked him to publish their books, so he started a small publishing company, *New Friends Publishing*. Others referred clients to him and the publishing business took off. He's now published books for numerous clients in the U.S., along with authors in Ireland and Peru.

Walker's incredible journey took him from high-school dropout to tile-setter to author to international publisher, all because he chose to follow his authentic self and let spirit take him where it would. And, his story didn't end there.

Watching Anne dabble with art, Walker found the process inspiring. Out of curiosity, he started experimenting with paints. His confidence had grown from his previous endeavors. After taking one pastel class, he painted a dog, which turned out so well, he painted more and began taking commissions to do pet portraits. One year after taking the pastel class, he won first- and third-place ribbons in a local art show.

All of these remarkable events with his books, publishing, and paintings happened within a six-year period because Walker chose to follow his authentic self and venture into the areas that called to him. He went against the traditional mind-set by being curious, without concern for failure, and doing impossible things simply because he was willing to give them a try. He said, "I found out I can do amazing things when I set my mind to it."

Can you relate to Layne Walker's story? Are you willing to let curiosity guide you to try new things without worrying about success, to really let yourself venture into the unknown? The spirit of adventure is how you will discover your authentic self.

Sam Walton, the creator of the Wal-Mart stores followed the same pattern of authenticity. Even after building a huge fortune serving rural America with his merchandising, he continued to motor around his hometown of Bentonville, Arkansas, in the same old pickup that he owned from the beginning.

Warren Buffet, the great businessman/investor, shows the same principle of authenticity. He made and invested millions, perhaps billions, by carefully researching industries and purchasing companies, yet he continues to live in his modest home in Nebraska, the same house he had lived in for decades before getting started.

If and when there are times you feel pulled this way and that, and you're not sure what you should do or who you should be, remember Will Rogers, Sam Walton, Layne Walker, and Warren Buffet. That might bring you back to the simplicity of your authentic self. Once you are centered in your realness, you will have a better sense of what direction is right for you.

In what areas of your life are you being authentic?

In what areas are you not being your authentic self? Why not?

What do you need to do to become authentic in all areas of your life?

Resilience: Walk on Hot Coals? No Problem

If you were to walk barefoot on hot sand, the skin on the bottom of your feet would be confused and frustrated, then respond by getting tougher. When the body gets stressed, it counters the stress by building up strength. Regardless of age, genetics, gender, race, or anything else, the human body responds to stress and replies by getting stronger. That is resilience.

San Francisco Psychologist Beth Miller has studied the quality of resiliency and found it to be like a muscle. The harder one works it, the stronger it gets. Her studies conclude that individuals who thrive under stress, while others fold, have gained certain skills.

Here are the skills that will help you gain strength when you are under stress:

- Admit your vulnerabilities. We all have them. No pretending.

- Find elements within the problem that you can deal with. Set up steps you can manage day-by-day. Think of this as eating an elephant one bite at a time. Just one bite each day!

- Develop communication skills. Become a connector. Connecting with others helps keep stress in perspective.

- Figure out what you need and go after it. Be resourceful. What are your core needs? Step away from habits and try something different. By taking a different approach, you can shake up your thinking and expand yourself.

- Acknowledge your talents and expertise. When times seem difficult, go with what is natural and easy for you. This will help you remember that there are things in your life that work just fine.

- Set limits and be clear about your boundaries. Be able to say, "No," and that includes admitting when you are pushing too hard.

- Forgive, forgive, forgive. Transform and release negative emotion. It saps energy and keeps you focused in the past. Be willing to admit your weaknesses. Forgiveness lifts and clears your energy. It opens you to solutions.

- Maintain your humor by seeing the absurdity in life. Laughing at yourself keeps you light and objective. It helps you keep your mind open for answers,

- Explore all possibilities, then persist. When you know what you want, you must also realize that there is a way to get it. Create time to contemplate possibilities.

- Find meaning in crisis. Cultivate a spiritual/philosophical approach because it adds a larger framework to life. There is a bigger purpose. How is this event helping you be stronger, more secure, more mature, better?

- Fully enter your suffering. You can accomplish this by sitting with the feeling. Beneath sadness or disappointment resides joy. By staying with the feeling, you will connect to something greater.

- Cultivate the ability to be alone and, at the same time, be willing to reach out to others. You are not in this alone. Learn how to rely on others. This connects your vulnerability and strength. There are those who believe that it is weak to ask for help, but it really shows strength. Trying to do everything alone when it is unnecessary, demonstrates ego-centric bravado and selfishness. You deny others the opportunity to support you.

We all know that stress is an everyday event in relationships, families, and careers. This list may help you pinpoint a method to release stress and become more resilient. Or, at the least, manage it.

One would have to say that Marchese Quglielo Marconi, the man who dreamed of harnessing the intangible forces of the ether, was resilient. When he announced to his friends that he had discovered a principle through which he could send messages through the air without the assistance of wires or other direct physical means of communication, they took him into custody and brought him to a psychiatric hospital. But Marconi was not crazy. He was a visionary.

Today, we credit this prophet with the means by which every television, radio, and cell phone is able to transfer messages through the air. His resiliency in continuing his work, despite naysayers, is the reason we can instantly send out news, information, and entertainment to every home, business, and country in the world. His great invention has helped shrink the world and has created a global community.

Dreamers, like Marconi, despite the disbelief of others, are to be credited with the astounding advancements that give each person an informational edge and speeds progress in our world. Marconi was outrageous and did the impossible.

Which of the above mentioned skills do you possess?

Which skills do you not possess?

Choose one of these skills and commit to strengthening it, then create a plan to do that. For instance, if you have problems asking for help, make a plan to do so.

Creative Imagination: How Does the Universe Want to Use Me Today?

Creative Imagination is an important quality that belongs to all outrageous people. You already have it, and as you read the following, you will find a great way to access it at a moment's notice.

Discovering people who use their creative imagination to solve simple problems is always inspiring. They give you the impression that, if *they* can do it, *you* can do it, too. Oftentimes success is the result of a simple idea that is tenaciously followed until there is a break-through. Frequently, these ideas can be conjured up by anyone. By becoming aware of potential ideas, you are encouraged to pay attention to what shows up in your mind. These concepts could be gold mines that offer the next bestseller, next great invention, or next new business opportunity.

On that note, there is a great story about a woman who worked in a Dallas bank.

In 1951, Bette Nesmith was happy to have her secretarial job that gleaned $300 a month, a decent salary at that time. However, one problem plagued her. She didn't know how to correct the mistakes she made with her new electric typewriter. Considering possibilities, she knew that artists could paint over their errors. Thus, she put together a concoction that she used to paint over her typing errors. Soon, all the secretaries in her building were using her invention.

Nesmith called her invention "Mistake Out." She attempted to sell it to various companies and marketing agencies but was turned away. Even IBM refused her product. Nevertheless, secretaries continued using her concoction, so she created a manufacturing facility in her kitchen and sold her product on her own.

Before long, orders began to flow in and she was able to hire a college student to help her. Neither of them had any sales experience. Plus, they were continually informed that "Mistake Out" was impractical. People just wouldn't use it to paint out their errors.

However, Nesmith kept manufacturing and selling her product anyway. Even though from August 1959 to April 1960, the company's expenses were $76 higher than the income, she didn't give up. She was working now as a part-time secretary and had saved up $200 to pay a chemist to develop a faster-drying formula.

With her new formula, she traveled throughout the country and sold the little white bottles. Her strategy was that, upon arriving in a town or city, she would get the local yellow pages and call every office-supply dealer. She visited stores and left a dozen bottles behind. Her orders grew. Soon, the Liquid Paper Corporation was born.

In 1979, when Bette Nesmith sold her company, she was earning $3.5 million annually on her little white bottles. By that time, her total yearly sales were $38 million. Her buyer, the Gillette Company, purchased Liquid Paper Corporation for $47.5 million. Not a bad return for an inventive secretary who sought to solve an everyday dilemma.

Everyone has creativity and inventiveness. Got any ideas that you need to follow up on?

Dr. Elmer R. Gates of Chevy Chase, Maryland, was prolific in creating useful patents. He became one of the great scientists in the world. In his years of cultivating and using his creative faculty, he produced more than 200 patents. He used a unique method to tap into his creative genius, a method that could be adopted by anyone desiring inspired results.

In his laboratory, Gates created what he termed his *personal communication room.* This was a soundproofed room, furnished meagerly with a table and a tablet on which to write. A push-button on the wall controlled the lighting. When he chose to tap into his creative imagination, he entered this room and turned off the lights. There, he concentrated on the invention he was developing. He would sit until ideas relative to his project began to flash across his mind.

There were occasions when his mind was so prolific, he wrote for hours. He wrote until his mind ran dry, so to speak.

Through this process, his creative imagination produced minute descriptions of ideas and principles that were not yet known to the scientific world. This was the manner in which he produced his patents. He basically made his living by *sitting for ideas*. He did this for some of the major corporations in America, as well.

Edison and Gates shared the use of this creative faculty, although each had their own way of accessing it. Edison made use of a cot situated in his laboratory. When he got stuck on a project, not sure what to do next, he would lie down on the cot and take a nap. He did this while holding a piece of metal. As he relaxed, the metal would drop from his hand and clink as it hit the floor. This would wake him from his sleep and he would write down the ideas that flowed from his mind. Genius has its ways.

The information that came through the minds of these great men superseded the reasoning mind's capacity. These thoughts came directly from Source, the Universe. In contrast, the intellect is incredibly limited in its supply. If you depend on reasoning alone, you are sometimes misled, since there is great disparage in how you perceive information, often tainted with the biases you hold. By working with your creative faculty, you open yourself to unlimited potential. It is your vast, unfettered, pure resource.

Creative imagination works by stimulating your mind so that you are reaching higher vibrational frequencies. This could be through meditation, affirmations, dreams, imagination, or sitting for ideas. Concentrate on the subject you wish to explore. This could be an idea or concept you are considering, or the solution to a problem. Hold a picture in your mind to represent that issue and sustain it until the subconscious mind takes over. Make sure you clear all other thoughts from your mind and patiently wait until the inspiration appears.

Creative imagination is vastly important for success in any venture. Be sure to cultivate it.

What subject would you like to *sit with* today?

Humor: It's Better to Laugh

It would be easy to toil at personal growth with a heavy, serious mind-set, but that would be missing the point. You must strive, instead, for lightness of attitude. That means look for humor, perhaps even silliness at times. If you examine masters and enlightened beings, you will note a quality of lightness, playfulness, and joy in their demeanor.

I once saw a photo of the Dalai Lama, the Spiritual Leader of Tibet, and South African Bishop Desmond Tutu. They were playing. Each had a twinkle in his eyes as they nudged each other like schoolboys. They exemplified the idea of looking at life lightly. You know the sayings: *This too shall pass* and *Accept what is.*

Humor keeps our energy light and our minds open. In the form of laughter, humor offers a wonderful way to heal ailments. No, I'm not referring to laugh pills, but there is a laugh therapy recently developed called "Laughter Yoga," which came from India and has spread across the U.S. and other countries. The participants join in fun exercises that promote laughter, relaxation, and deep breathing. Even if this is not available to you, you can create your own laugh therapy.

It has been proven that laughter can heal maladies. Humor and laughter elevate your spirit. When you exist in high energy, your body innately shifts into its natural rhythm and healing takes place.

People have actually overcome serious illnesses through the use of comedy. In his book, *Anatomy of an Illness,* author Norman

Cousins described the method he used. When diagnosed with a terminal illness, he watched old films like "The Three Stooges" and "Abbot and Costello." He laughed himself to health.

Laughing at silly flicks allows tension, depression, and suppressed negativity to release. It's a bit like taking a mini-vacation. Your mind takes a break from worries. It opens to becomes spacious. Humor also lets you see another side of life, to form a new perspective. By letting go of heaviness, intensity, and smallness, you might even laugh at yourself.

Think about it. Every situation has a humorous component. Comedians make fortunes dramatizing the funny side of life. You, too, can become an observer and catch the humor. Do your own laugh therapy. Stand back, become objective, and instead of looking at how bad things are, train yourself to see the absurdity.

One of my favorite observations is watching people run to the grocery store when the weather forecasters predict snow. It is as though they are planning on spending the winter in a cave. They buy huge stocks of bread and milk. Of course, the next day, the snowplows are out and the roads are clear. I wonder what they do with all that bread and milk.

There is almost nothing more indispensable when dealing with people than humor. Having humor doesn't particularly mean cracking jokes. Humor is the ability to experience setbacks while comprehending that the world has not come to an end. When you don't take yourself or your situation too seriously, you'll do better in any and all endeavors.

There is a laugh point in every circumstance. Often it is *you.*

Observe the way people manipulate each other, or themselves. They use guilt and intimidation. Lots of folks fall for it. On the other hand, a smiling, cheerful leader conveys more confidence and wins more cooperation than a negative, gloomy one.

When you view life's games objectively, it is quite humorous. I wonder what would happen if someone said, "I'm not playing your games." It is a choice.

Of course, this is how many folks avoid responsibility. "It is your fault. You made me do it." Or they get so carried away with the details of an event, they miss the point entirely. That can be funny. Then there is politics. Sit back, watch the tactics. It is a show to be enjoyed.

The truth is you have no control over others' actions, but they will surely bear the consequences of them. You may as well notice what is going on and see it as a game.

For your part, endeavor to grasp a bigger picture. Ask yourself what is really happening. What is this really all about? Keeping the purpose of an event in mind allows you to recognize the silliness of it, be it actions or reactions, even your own, for that matter. In fact, particularly your own.

Enjoying life keeps you healthy and peaceful. You are living in Light energy. How many happy people have you seen with serious illnesses? Be clear. I'm not referring to clowns who crack jokes to hide insecure egos, but well-adjusted individuals who don't go off the deep end over inconsequential concerns. They maintain perspective and play it all as a game.

Laugher and joy are health-producing stimulants. Joy increases circulation. Laughter shakes your body, loosening and soothing tense nerves and muscles. When you are having fun, your brain emits endorphins. It is good for you. Fun allows body parts to return to their natural rhythm and full-functioning capabilities. There is no muscular resistance to inhibit natural flows and processes. Healing can take place.

As you let go of worry, anxiety, and heaviness, you revert back to your natural state of *joy!* Think of a baby who smiles over the simplest things, or a puppy that goes into convulsive happy tail-wagging when you acknowledge its presence. Lightness in our energy, our mood, and our outlook on life, that is what we seek.

Humor is a most important quality to cultivate. That doesn't necessarily mean telling jokes or funny stories. Rather, it refers to the ability to accept the twists and turns life throws your way with dignity and knowing that the world will not end if you don't get your way. If you don't take yourself, or shall I say your *ego*, too seriously, your chances of achieving the results you desire increase. Plus, you free up time. Guarding your ego, lest it be wounded, is time-consuming and tedious. It keeps you bogged down and closed.

When you take yourself too seriously, you set yourself up for hurt. If things don't go your way, if there is a negative setback, if someone doesn't like you, it can seem like the end of the world. You can waste a lot of time and energy worrying about things over which you have little control. Protecting a fragile ego limits accomplishment, learning, and moving forward. Just be ready to laugh.

Every circumstance offers a chance to giggle or, at least, evoke a smile. Can you laugh at yourself? This does not mean being self-demeaning or self-effacing. Can you laugh at your own antics and ego needs?

Even when problems are serious, exaggeration builds drama. It never helps. Step back and observe how the news media generates fear. When you look objectively, you can watch the manipulation without taking it personally. As you take yourself and the world lightly, your situations will improve and your happiness will expand. Let go of your mental heaviness so there is room for solutions to appear.

When a setback occurs, instead of reacting, use your newly built muscles of objectivity to view it with detachment. Breathing space will allow a new direction or alternative to present itself. Locking down options limits you. Humor keeps your mind flexible.

By maintaining equilibrium, a sense of proportion, and humor in a crisis, others are able to trust and rely on you. Because they respect your calm demeanor, they ultimately demonstrate better performance, loyalty, and appreciation. Contributing calmness is far better than adding confusion and panic. This process can be as simple as the willingness to hold a positive view and smiling.

Abraham Lincoln served as a great model of leadership under pressure. In one tension-filled moment, he said, "Gentlemen, why don't you laugh? With the fearful strain that is upon me night and day, if I did not laugh, I should die." Like Lincoln, most of us have discovered humor is the way to relieve stress.

Even though some problems are quite serious, it doesn't help to exaggerate their implications. With lightness, your circumstances will improve and you'll have more to be happy about. An old saying is, "The two hardest things to handle in life are failure and success." Both are easier managed with humor.

The happiest people don't necessarily have the best of everything. They just *make* the best of everything. The Buddhists say, "Laughter is the language of the Gods."

Try these two exercises:

- Pick out three areas of your life that seem burdensome or heavy. Look at these situations from every angle, and find a way to bring light to your perspective. It is not about laughing at what is going on, but about learning to see with different eyes. It is about moving out of victim-mentality to see the possibilities or opportunities. Ask for vision.
- Create opportunities to laugh. Make sure you laugh every day.

Belief: Make the Universe Your Servant

Years ago, the Saint Louis Zoo was one of the first zoological parks to take animals out of cages and put them in big pits. They started with the bears.

A visitor noted a big polar bear pacing rhythmically forward twenty feet and then backing up twenty feet, then repeating the action again and again. The visitor inquired of the zoo keeper, "Why does the bear pace back and forth in that small area? It has a great big pit to move about in?

The keeper replied, "He has the Small Cage Habit. This animal was born and raised in captivity in a twenty-foot cage. He got his exercise by pacing forward and back in the cage. So, even though he was moved to a much larger area, he continues to exercise by pacing twenty feet forward and back.

Many people have the Small Cage Habit and resist change in the same way the bears did. They can be surrounded with possibilities, ideas, innovations, and resources, but continue to do things the same tired, old way, not bothering to familiarize themselves with fresh and better methods. They are intimidated with expansion and newness, believing that the old way provides stability. And they have their reasons. "I've always done it this way. I am comfortable with this method. I don't know how to do it any other way." These are all ways of saying, "I have the Small Cage Habit and I am not interested in growing or exploring other possibilities."

Growth demands new ways, new ideas, new thinking, and new methods. It all starts with belief. Belief that it is possible. Belief you can do it. Belief you can learn.

Recently, I spoke to a woman who works in finance. Because she has expanded her consciousness, she is now shifting her work to larger, wealthier, more progressive clients and businesses. She has moved from small-minded, victim-type people to those who see and operate from a bigger picture. This would not be happening if she had not grown and expanded her own mind-set to believe in greater outcomes. Some would say that personal and spiritual growth is frivolous, but this woman defies that reasoning.

The question to you is, are you operating from the Small Cage Habit or from an expanded understanding of greater possibilities? Are you ready to step into the unknown and expand your potential, or are you trying to be safe in your old ways? Are you ready to believe you can be more and have more?

Henry David Thoreau often indicated that *belief* in an enterprise is the one thing that is fundamental to its success. Thus, if you have a goal, believe that you can attain it. Believe that you are, even now, in the process of attainment.

What is belief? Is a thought that has been repeated so many times that you have adopted it as your own. That means, at any time, you can create a new belief. For instance, what about the idea that you are talented and significant and have a meaningful purpose? Repeat this idea over and over until it becomes a belief. It will make doing the impossible become a matter of course.

There are many stories of people who had come up from poverty to achieve great success in life. They all started with a determined resolution or a belief.

One woman tells a story about her family who was so poor that people often brought them food baskets. As a little girl, she felt humiliated that her father couldn't support them. She would hide and cry bitterly. At that early age, she decided that her goal was to be successful. And she did it. Poverty can be a great motivator. It has probably helped to make more people outrageously successful than any other one factor.

James Cash Penney, the great merchant and founder of the J.C. Penney stores, was the seventh of twelve children. At eight years old, he started raising pigs to earn money for his clothes. He professed that one of the great motivators in his life was adversity. Hardship taught him to never give up, always start over, keep his faith strong, and realize that adversity can make a person strong.

Another fellow, Al Haake, suffered from acute stuttering. Children laughed at him in school. They called him out in baseball games, just to hear him stutter. It was demoralizing to him. Then, one afternoon, he heard a U.S. senator speak. The senator said, "Look, you can do anything you want to do, if you believe in yourself."

Al Haake wanted to believe he could speak clearly. He read about a famous man named Demosthenes who put pebbles in his mouth to overcome his stammering. Haake did the same and, like Demosthenes, became a great speaker. He was employed by General Motors Corporation to speak throughout the country. He held people spellbound by his clarity, articulation, message, and beauty of speech. He proved the senator's promise to be accurate.

An interesting thing about belief is that, when you truly believe, you become rock solid about that belief. By holding your mind in a lock-pattern to reach your goal, the Universe has no alternative but to provide the means and opportunity to fulfill your belief.

Another young man, Dave Thomas, grew up in poverty and lacked an education. When he landed a job with Colonel Harlan Sanders selling fried chicken, he saw Sanders to be a great man and a loveable person. This observation of Sanders was enhanced one day when Thomas was given the opportunity to be in attendance at the Waldorf-Astoria Hotel in New York where Dr. Norman Vincent Peale awarded Sanders the Horatio Alger Award. In his speech, Peale acknowledged that Colonel Sanders had no money at all when he developed the Kentucky Fried Chicken business.

Upon hearing of Sanders' disadvantage, Thomas made a commitment. "That was when I decided that, one day, I too would receive this award. I saw myself standing on a platform with Dr. Peale giving me the award. But, I didn't want to sell fried chicken. I wanted to sell hamburgers."

With little more than a belief and a vision, Dave Thomas set about creating the giant fast-food restaurant chain called Wendy's. Later, when he was asked the secret of his success, he said, "Give quality and believe you can." Perseverance and belief truly are analogous to success.

Nineteenth-century physicist, Marie Curie, said, "Life is not easy for any of us; but what of that? We must have perseverance and, above all, confidence in ourselves. We must believe that we are gifted for something and that this thing, at whatever cost, must be attained."

What are your goals and dreams?

Perhaps it is time to envision them and take action as did Thomas, Sanders, Penney, and Curie did. With perseverance and belief, you can move past limitations. Start with the most obvious step and go from there. Every day, do something to stay your course. Each step you take, no matter how small, moves you closer to achievement. Believe you can while you keep your eye on the goal.

Objectivity: Life Is a Movie. Wonder What Is Playing Today?

There is a general tendency to view mistakes as terrible, rather than as inexperience being at play. Perhaps the idea is to have immediate, perfect results instead of recognizing that expertise comes with practice and determination.

When a rocket is blasted into space, radar determines whether it hits or misses its target. If the rocket does not connect with its target, adjustments are made to modify the projectory for the next one. In fact, for most of the rocket's journey, it is off-course. The technical exercise is to continually correct the rocket's path so that it hits its mark. The technicians in charge don't care how many modifications have to be made. They are concentrating on reaching their destination as the ultimate objective. This is the perfect definition of objectivity: calculating what is necessary to reach a goal without emotion or prejudice.

Viewing your journey in the same manner makes change possible. Perhaps it makes sense to review your progress periodically to determine if you are on the right path. Or, is it necessary to alter your course or choose a different target? With consistent effort, you will arrive at your designated outcome. Reevaluating objectively without negative judgment or condemnation facilitates progress. Criticism impedes it.

Apply this principle to learning any new skill. It could be cooking, dancing, singing, accounting, communicating, golfing, investing, or relating to people. Each area necessitates practice. With practice comes success.

As I searched for a story that would illustrate objectivity, I came upon the tale of George Washington Carver. Carver has always been a favorite of mine because he started life with the handicap of being a slave. He broke through the barriers that went with that position. Through hard work, he advanced to become a great scientist.

It was through his efforts in developing multiple uses for the peanut that he is renowned. As a result of his labor, he is given almost sole responsibility for the rise in U.S. peanut production after the boll weevil devastated the American cotton crop in 1892. He literally saved the Southern farmers by creating adaptations and planting crops that would work in the depleted soil. Plus, his plants offered nutritional food to the farmers' families.

You will note that whenever Carver's path seemed blocked by events or race prejudice, he found a way to continue his journey. He typifies flexibility and objectivity. Throughout, he was true to his purpose, which was education and botany. He kept his focus without taking on the anger, resentment, or smallness of prejudice, even for those who attempted to harm him.

Here is his story. See if it inspires you as it has me.

In the mid 1850's, George Washington Carver was born a slave in the area now known as Diamond, Missouri. The exact day and year of his birth are unknown. His master, Moses Carver, was a German-American immigrant who had purchased George's parents, Mary and Giles, on October 9, 1855 for $700.

When George was one week old, night raiders from Arkansas kidnapped him, along with a sister and his mother. George's older brother, James, was rushed to safety from the kidnappers. The outlaws sold the slaves in Kentucky. Moses Carver hired John Bentley to find them, but he was only able to locate the infant George. Moses negotiated with the raiders and gained the boy's return.

When slavery was abolished, Moses Carver and his wife Susan raised George and James as their own children. They encouraged George to continue his intellectual pursuits and *Aunt Susan* taught him the basics of reading and writing.

Inasmuch as black people were not allowed at the public school in Diamond Grove, George traveled ten miles south to Neosho to the black children's school. When he arrived, the school was closed for the night, so he slept in a nearby barn.

The next morning, he met a kind woman, Mariah Watkins, with whom he asked to rent a room. When he identified himself as "Carver's George," as he had done his whole life, she replied that from now on his name was to be George Carver. Watkins' said to him, "You must learn all you can, then go back out into the world and give your learning back to the people."

This thought impressed him greatly.

At age thirteen, he relocated to another foster family so that he could attend the academy at Fort Scott, Kansas. It was there that he witnessed the murder of a black man by a group of whites. As a result, Carver left the city. He attended a series of other schools, finally earning his diploma at Minneapolis High School in Minneapolis, Kansas.

After graduation, he was rejected admission to Highland College in Highland, Kansas because of his race. Consequently, in1886, Carver traveled by wagon to Eden Township in Ness County, Kansas, where he homesteaded a claim and maintained a small conservatory of plants, flowers, and a geological collection. He manually plowed his seventeen acres and planted a variety of crops, fruit trees, forest trees, and shrubbery.

Throughout his life, Carver was drawn to education and botany. Various people encouraged him along the way. He attended Simpson College in Indianola, Iowa, and Iowa State Agricultural College in Ames where he was the first black student. As a result of his research in plant pathology and mycology at the Iowa Experiment Station, he gained national recognition and respect as a botanist. This led to Carver being the first black faculty member at Iowa State.

Later, in 1896, Booker T. Washington, the president of the Tuskegee Institute, invited Carver to head its Agriculture Department. Carver found a home there and taught for forty-seven years, developing the department into a strong research center. It was through Carver's hard work and research that he developed hundreds of adaptations for the peanut, which allowed southern farmers to come back after the devastation of their main crop of cotton.

When I read stories like this, I am awed by the person's ability to look beyond his circumstances and find his way. Life most definitely bestows great blessings when one is ready to receive them.

With fortitude and focus, an unlikely individual in the person of a slave, moved past all the incredible obstacles that faced him and became a renowned scientist. He supplied the research that saved the very people who considered him less valuable than themselves. Throughout, he did not participate in the prejudice that ruled the times in which he lived.

This story puts things into proper perspective. We have so much opportunity today. The prospect of exploring the wealth of our own minds, to make significant contributions, and to lead fulfilling lives is daunting.

George Washington Carver is a wonderful example of what is possible when one objectively chooses to survive challenges and conflict in order to follow an inherent path. Because he kept his focus, Carver was able to share his incredible research. Would the agricultural industry have received his knowledge had it not been devastated by the boll weevil? No one knows. Nevertheless, George Washington Carver looked beyond racial barriers and shared his gift with all who would receive it.

In the manner of George Washington Carver, your life will get easier when you establish an objective view. This means to accept without prejudice, tension, or pressure each situation as it comes. Respond to events by flowing with them, by doing what comes naturally. Responding, rather than reacting, helps you perceive the opportunity at hand.

To become objective, step back as though you are viewing a movie or dream. How do you want it to culminate? What would encourage that ending? What can you do or not do?

Recognize that you have physical, not psychological limitations. You can train yourself to be objective. It takes practice. You must be willing to set your ego aside to view your situation as it truly is. Then your choices become clear:

Use these practices to develop objectivity:

- Remember an emergency situation of the past and how you took charge. What was the feeling? Practice creating that same feeling daily in all that you do.

- Hesitate before reacting. Ask yourself, what are my options and what are the results of each option?

- Practice being sensitive to others' feelings. Ask yourself why they feel or think as they do.

- Practice seeing life as a movie. Anticipate the ending in each scenario. Is this conclusion logical, given all the factors? In time, your accuracy will increase along with your objectivity.

With practice, you can develop a stable, objective outlook that allows life to serve you rather than you serving it.

Gratitude: Nectar of the Gods

One of the great laws of prosperity is gratitude. Gratitude sounds simple. Yet often, it is not practiced. When most people gaze around and perceive all they have accomplished, both tangible and intangible, instead of feeling awed and appreciative, they frequently think, "Is that all?" Or, " But I don't have that thing, event, or relationship I want." Or, "What's next?" In other words, stopping to smell the roses is not part of their repertoire.

Stop and think, do you consciously appreciate your friends, family, home, job, freedom, health, the money you have, or the money you have earned? It is easy to take these things for granted and think that what you possess isn't good enough or enough. You might be saying, "My car isn't a Rolls Royce. It's an old Ford. I'm not president of the company. I'm only a low-level supervisor. I don't make enough money. I don't have enough prestige, live in the 'best' part of town, or know the 'right' people."

The attention here is not on what you have achieved, but on what you do *not* have, on what is missing, on what you might see as bad rather than what is good in life. This is called *fear-based thinking*. You never win or feel good about yourself when you live in fear and focus on lack.

Appreciate, instead, that the old car transports you wherever you want to go. Your current job is a stepping-stone to wherever you go from here. The house you own represents the down-payment on the next one. All your past learning experiences graduate you to the next level and prepare you for greater expression and service. You will more easily move to a new car, job, home, and elevated opportunities, by appreciating the ones you've already had. If you value your present job position and the customers you have, the new customers will more readily present themselves.

One month after Wil Smith (no, not the movie star) and his girlfriend broke up, she informed him she was pregnant. Will stated he would do whatever he had to do to take care of the baby. At the time Olivia was born, Wil was in the Navy. He knew that if he stayed in the service, he would always be leaving his daughter on deployment. So, he left the Navy and was accepted at Bowdoin College.

When Olivia was around ten months old, her mother was having a difficult time and reached a breaking point. Will realized that the best thing for Olivia was to take care of her himself.

During his first semester at Bowdoin, he lived off-campus with a roommate and held a cleaning job at Staples at night. Sometimes he took the baby to work with him and hid her in the closet. Being honest with himself, Wil admitted he wasn't ready for college. He later said to his daughter, "Had I not been able to kiss you good night every night before studying, I would not have had the strength to do it. There were times when the only way I could get through was to check in on you and see you sleeping, then go back to my studies."

In his second semester, a woman who worked at Bowdoin helped him move to campus housing. Even though he was the first single father raising a child on campus, things were finally getting better.

Wil was grateful to know that Olivia was with him and safe. He appreciated that she was easy to care for. She was quiet, didn't bother anyone, and adapted to school right away. Wil brought her to class, gave her crayons and other things to do, and Olivia sat sit at a desk and kept herself entertained.

Olivia's first babysitters were Wil's basketball teammates. He would come from class and find four giant guys and his eighteen-month-old child tearing up the room. He trusted those guys with Olivia.

When Will graduated, he carried Olivia in his arms to get his diploma. "They called both of our names. All my classmates stood up and cheered. They gave me the only standing ovation of the day."

As Wil describes it, having Olivia was a drastic change in his life, but it was the best thing that ever happened to him. He told Olivia, "I felt like before you came along, my mother, my guardian angel who passed away on my fifteenth birthday, was looking down from heaven and got tired of me drifting through the universe and said, 'God, please do something. Send that boy someone to take care of.'"

Wil tells that when he was present in the delivery room at Olivia's birth, "I physically felt something go into my heart. It was a feeling of completeness that I hadn't felt since my mother had passed."

This gratitude has spread to Olivia, as well. She came home from school to take care of her father when he was sick. She said, "That first week, when I was home from school, I would cook you dinner, and it made me happy being able to care for you, knowing that my whole life, you were doing that for me. You're my rock."

Wil and Olivia Smith personify gratitude. Gratitude for each other, for the opportunity to make a difference, to offer care, and to really love.

Living in gratitude is a law of nature. When you accept and are at peace with your current status, things begin to change naturally, easily. Deep, sincere gratitude sows the seeds that blossom in abundance. This is a principle of nature and it is magnetic. When people feel acknowledged and appreciated by you, they more readily acknowledge and appreciate you. When you are grateful for all you have and all you have experienced, even the seemingly bad stuff, your life expands.

Gratitude is an elevated energy. When you feel it, you are also elevated. Everyone can experience gratitude whenever they want. Look to all that is beautiful and let go of that which seems imperfect. Your mind is pliable. Decide where you want to focus it. To magnetize abundance, joy, love, health, and all good things to you, live in an attitude of gratitude.

This is how you do it. Instead of focusing on what isn't working, give some love and attention to the things that are. Take a mental inventory of all the things, events, people, and opportunities for which you are grateful. With consistent practice, you will notice that the negative way of thinking will begin to shift. You'll be able to experience the happiness that is waiting for you.

Here is an exercise: Begin each morning with appreciation for everything and all possibilities. As you do this, expand your feeling so that this sense of gratitude fills the room. Then, end your day with gratitude for all you have experienced and all the ways you have given and received. Again, expand your energy.

When you sleep with this high energy, your mind will be working through the night on all the ways to bring abundance into your life. As you do this exercise, make sure you have at least five things on your gratitude list, morning and evening, and keep adding to the list. Your energy will expand and soar!

Oprah Winfrey keeps a gratitude journal where she daily acknowledges everyone and everything for which she is grateful. It works for her. Her life is abundant.

Hey, what a great world we live in. We have endless opportunities to express, try things out, experience, experiment, live freely, laugh, love, share, and enjoy all sorts of abundance. I'm grateful. Are you?

Let's Work It Out

Here are some questions regarding each of the characteristics for success listed in this chapter. These questions are meant to open your mind and give you the opportunity to explore new ideas and new attitudes that will lead to greater understanding of yourself and help you move forward in achieving the impossible.

Persistence
- What are the challenges you currently face?
- What is each challenge attempting to teach you? Keep this positive.

Courage
- Is there a value that you hold dear, that you would inconvenience yourself to fight for, encourage, or support?

- Have you ever put your own well-being in jeopardy because you believed something else was more important?
- Do you or have you ever perceived something of such great significance that you were willing to risk your good standing in deference to it?
- What risk are you willing to take now? For what purpose?

Optimism

- What situation in your life do you need to give new meaning? Can you reinterpret its value to your growth?
- How can you increase your optimism?
- In what area of life do you want to be more optimistic?
- Name a current challenge where you would be willing to envision a positive outcome. Good! Name another one.

Enthusiasm

- How do you express enthusiasm? About what?
- What area of your life needs more enthusiasm?

Authenticity

- How do you demonstrate authenticity?
- In what area would you like to be more authentic?

Resilience

- How do you show vulnerability and to whom?
- What do you do to relieve stress?
- Where and with whom do you need to set stronger boundaries?
- Who and what do you need to forgive?
- When was the last time you asked for help?
- Is there anyone you need to ask for help at this time?

Creative Imagination
- What is your method to call on your creative imagination?
- What projects, issues, or solutions would you like to focus on today with your creative imagination?

Humor
- Can you laugh at your own foibles?
- What way can you lighten up and bring more laughter into your life?

Belief
- What is your strongest positive belief about your capabilities?
- In what way can you strengthen that belief?
- Are you willing to let go of self-criticism and negative self-talk? When?
- Of which achievements are you most proud?

Objectivity
- What area of your life do you need to view more objectively?
- If your life is a movie, what do you see as the main plot? As the theme?

Gratitude
- List at least five items, things, or people for which you can feel gratitude right now.
- What present circumstances that appear negative to you, can you reverse with feelings of gratitude? What can these circumstances offer you?
- Pick one person in your life for whom you have felt irritation or down-right anger or resentment. Choose to be grateful that the person chose to show up to help you learn a lesson.

The mind, when stretched to a new level,
can never go back to its original condition.

—Oliver Wendell Holmes, Poet and Author

It's not what people say or do to you …
it's your self-talk that determines how you feel.
It's not about them. It's about you. You have the power
to create the life you have always wanted.
Choose to listen to yourself, not others!

—Jack Canfield, Author and Speaker

■

Chapter Ten

To Have More, Be More

Expand Your Greatness

There is a story about a fellow in New York who had friends from a small town visit him. The visitors were amazed at the seeming chaos and massive activity of the city. They thought it was too loud, confusing, and ugly. The host decided to give his guests another point of view. He took them to the top of the Empire State Building and asked them to look out over the city. As they peered across the grand spectacle, they were awed with its magnificence. The colors, the lights, the movement, and life poured through the streets like a grand symphony. Their opinion of New York changed in that moment.

Changing your perspective is an important skill to cultivate for personal growth. It is about learning to look with different eyes. You can easily become mired in archaic ideas that are irrelevant and false. It helps to pretend you are ten feet tall, looking out over life. You can more readily identify truth from falsehood. That doesn't mean to grow your physical body. It does mean to raise your perception.

Have you had an experience, like an illness, a divorce, a downsizing at work, or a bad investment, that seemed negative at the moment? Then, as time passed, you realized that the experience was a turning point and a blessing. That is an example of looking with different eyes. You are seeing the bigger picture.

Once, I was being interviewed on a national radio station and the host made a comment about my *failed marriage*. I never thought that my marriage that ended in divorce was a failure. From my point of view, I thought it was successful. I grew up during that marriage. I had four beautiful children and the opportunity to raise them. I learned about responsibility, dependability, and unconditional love. I had met the challenge of family life. So I responded to the host, "My marriage wasn't a failure. It was a huge success, and when it was time for us to go our separate ways, we did."

To say the least, the host was shocked. He had never thought of the end of a marriage in those terms.

The thought process of success or failure can stunt a person's development. We must guard against small-compartmentalized thinking. It keeps many people stuck in ineffective patterns that block growth.

To have more, you must be more. It is imperative to stretch your vision and perspective. There is always a strategy to get things done. There are multiple ways to turn a negative into a positive. Here are some examples.

Mongol leader Genghis Khan achieved a victory over China by employing the talents of one individual. For centuries, the Great Wall of China rebuffed the Mongols as the wall could not be breached. But Khan looked beyond the ordinary methods of gaining entry.

One night, a simple shepherd approached the drunken guard stationed at the city gate. The shepherd promised the guard rewards for permission to gain entry. As the shepherd entered the city, hordes of Khan's troops came with him. Khan's simple plan, using one lone shepherd, took down the Great Wall of China. He looked at the problem from a different perspective.

Another instance goes back to World War II when Russia was an ally. After the war, there was a celebration planned in New York where representatives of all the U.S. allies were invited. All responded but Russia.

Walter Hoving, President of Bonwit Teller and the Fifth Avenue Association, did not appreciate Stalin's brush-off. Hoving's reaction was to send a cable to Stalin and his outrage that Russia did not choose to join with the other nations.

Less than a day later, he received a personal response from Stalin, asserting that a representative would be present for the ceremony.

One small action on Hoving's part made the difference. He did not think that Stalin, being the leader of a great country, would not be approachable. No, he had a different vision and was willing to act on the idea of unity among allies.

When it comes to interesting ways to solve a problem, Lynn Zwerling might win the prize. In late 2009, Zwerling stood in front of 600 male prisoners at the Pre-Release Prison Unit in Jessup, Maryland. Her opening line was "Who wants to knit?" The burly men were taken back with the idea, but Lynn Zwerling assured them that men had invented the craft.

Nearly two years later, Zwerling and her associates had instructed more than 100 prisoners to knit, while dozens more waited to take her weekly class. "I have guys that have never missed one time in two years," comments Zwerling. "Some have reported that they miss dinner to come to class."

Even though the men were reluctant at first, complaining that knitting was too girly or difficult, they yielded to a five-minute knitting lesson and, as Zwerling puts it, "The men found Zen and became hooked."

It had taken Zwerling five years before her idea was accepted by the warden, because the Warden worried about freely handing out knitting needles to prisoners who had been convicted of violent crimes. Nonetheless, Assistant Warden Margaret Chippendale is on record for saying that the men involved with knitting got into trouble less often. "It's very positive," she says, "because you can see when you go into the room, the dynamics of their conversation: very calm, very soothing. It radiates, even when they leave the room and go out into the institution."

Ricky Horton, 38, served almost four years at the Pre-Release Prison Unit. He reluctantly joined the knitting class six months prior to release. Horton's first reaction was that he wasn't going to do *that thing.* "And then I went to class and you were actually speaking to real people. People can't really understand that in prison you're completely separated from anything normal or real in the world. You're always told what to do and when to do it, so to have people come in and treat you like a human being means so much. They came in and they were like my mom."

The men started by knitting comfort dolls, which they gave to children removed from their homes because of domestic issues. Then, they moved on to hats for kids at the inner-city elementary school.

Each week, the men eagerly await the women's arrival and promptly get to work. "It takes you away a little," Horton says. "You have to watch what you're doing, otherwise your stitches will become loose or tight or you'll skip stitches. It almost makes you feel like you don't have to be anything. You're all sitting there knitting. You can just be yourself."

Ricky Horton is a success story. He was released from prison and currently works in construction. He believes that his involvement with the knitting group helped him get paroled because it demonstrated to the parole interviewers his willingness to supply positive effort to help the community. He continues to keep in touch with the women instructors and is currently knitting a beaded scarf. "They're not normal people. They're almost like saints."

The knitting class started with Lynn Zwerling's desire to share her passion of knitting, and from there, a revolutionary change occurred in the tough environment of prison, with men who knew little about community, sharing, or calmness. Magic happens in strange ways and even stranger places. By offering her class to prisoners, Zwerling and her crew get to be more and help their students be more, as well. Everyone walks away richer.

Rosa Parks is another example of an individual operating from a different perspective. In December, 1955, after a long day at work, Parks rode home in a full bus in Alabama and chose to sit in the *white section.* That was the only seat available at the time. According to law, a black person was required to give up her seat for a white person. Parks chose not to do that. What followed was her arrest, imprisonment, Montgomery's bus boycott, and the beginning of the Civil Rights Movement.

Parks' belief that she had as much right to sit on that bus as any other paid rider generated a revolutionary wave that was felt throughout the nation. Rosa Parks offered her life courageously and became an icon for individual freedom.

We have within us the ability to be bigger than our circumstances and to think outside the box. We have the power to affect change. Each of these examples illustrates our ability to look beyond an obstacle and find another way.

Now, let's bring this to the personal level. List a few instances in your life that appeared challenging. This could be the end of a relationship, death of a close friend or loved one, job change, injury, illness, or accident.

Challenging Experiences

1.

2.

3.

4.

Examine each incident. Ask yourself: What was the blessing in each situation? How did I grow? Perceive the event as though you were standing on the Empire State Building. In other words, look from a higher perspective. How did I transform as a result of this situation? How was I made stronger ? What power or wisdom did I develop?

Take your time and reflect on these questions. Life is constantly providing us with opportunities to be more and have more. When we grasp the larger meaning of an event, we are changed forever.

One person I know was wrongfully fired from a tenured engineering job because of a mix-up in parts supplied to a customer. He grieved for a while, then realized this was his chance to start his own technology business, which he did. His business thrived and was exceedingly prosperous. Additionally, he gained the free time he desired so he could travel. This would not have happened had he not been fired.

A woman I know left a long, abusive marriage. In her relationship, she was bullied and beaten. In her divorce, she lost all her material possessions. Yet, with the peace she had gained by being away from her abusive husband, her self-esteem increased and her emotional wounds healed. She ultimately met a wonderful, considerate, supportive man and formed a great new partnership with him. Later, she wrote a book about her former, narcissistic husband and the marital abuse she endured. Through her recovery process, she was able to help many other women.

Another man I knew contracted a terminal illness. He told me that it was truly a blessing for him in that he finally took down his walls and did what he'd always wanted to do. He became a clown, fulfilling his life's dream. In his process of dying, he became more and learned how to live.

In every relationship and work experience I have had, I learned great lessons in how to work with people, how to communicate, present ideas, negotiate, manage meetings and events, as well as how to create peace in turmoil and calm others in the process.

We learn through our experiences. We may not be able to dictate all of our circumstances, but we can control our reactions to them. Teach yourself to look deeper and higher so that you are constantly enriched with new insight and wisdom. To have more you must be more.

Business leader Jim Rohn stated it this way, "If you want to be wealthy and happy, learn this lesson well. Learn to work harder on yourself than you do on your job."

Most people will buy a great computer, IPod, cell phone, filing system, and software for their business activities, but don't stock the most important items in their arsenal in order to be successful and attract the right opportunities. Important items include the right attitudes and beliefs. For most people, personal growth lies far down the priority list. Material conquests, like the big house, exotic travel, wealth, and position or status, are the big attention grabbers, yet no one can achieve any of these things without first developing insight, wisdom, patience, determination, and self-knowledge. Actually, the most challenging assignment in life is personal development, and guess what? It provides dividends and rewards for the duration of your entire life.

If material acquisition is your goal, the only way to accomplish it is by developing yourself. That means the person you become is far more important than what you acquire. What you become and what you achieve are magically linked. Look at it this way, who you are has made it possible to have what you have, good or bad. Income rarely surpasses personal development.

If you want more, you must be prepared to handle more responsibility and give more. If you're afraid to make decisions, take a risk, look foolish, or invest time and/or money in your progress, you've limited how far you will go. The prerequisite to building or maintaining the energy necessary to attract the right people and opportunities is expanding your personal potential. Again, personal growth.

Growing your potential means understanding and taking responsibility for your needs and behaviors. There can be no blaming, whining, finger-pointing, running from conflict, or hiding when things get tough. It means accepting that you have a role to play in the Universe, something that you can do better than anyone else, and making it your business to figure out what that is. Discovering your uniqueness and working it for all it's worth is how it's done.

Mahatma Gandhi said it this way. "Become the change you desire."

Buddha asserted, "Your work is to discover your work and give yourself to it."

Jim Rohn stated, "Unless you change how you are, you'll always have what you've got."

This is to say, to have more, be more.

What are your challenges? In what way can they help you expand? What is your next goal? What do you have to become to meet it? How can you use your life right now to be the person you want to be?

These are the right questions. Go for it!

*A leader has the vision and conviction
that a dream can be achieved.
He inspires the power and energy to get it done.*
—Ralph Lauren, Designer

*There is an advantage in every disadvantage
and a gift in every problem.*
—John Johnson,
American Businessman and Publisher

■

Chapter Eleven

Set Your Intention

If you don't like the idea of others controlling you or running your life, you better set your own intentions. Your ability to choose your intentions is the most important freedom you have. It is through the faculty of determining your intentions that you set the tone of your life.

Every event and circumstance is essentially neutral. You get to decide its relevance and the value you give it. For example, the employee who loses his job can recognize a chance to move on to something greater, choose to create something new, or be a victim. The loss of a loved one can create a terminal emptiness or the opportunity to remember joyously the gifts shared in the relationship.

Suze Orman is a famous example of someone changing tracks when hardship struck. In 1980, Orman was a waitress looking to start her own restaurant. She wanted to safeguard her investment money and, knowing little about money management or investing, she sought advice from a Merrill Lynch representative. She met a broker and placed her money into an account with the company. Although she had told him that she only made $400 a week and needed to keep her money safe, the broker chose to pursue the risky strategy of buying options. He told her that she could make "a quick $100 a week" and had her sign a blank form giving him control over her funds. The plan worked well at first, but she ended up losing all her money within three months.

After losing her money, Orman researched all she could find about money management and decided to become a broker. She applied to the same Merrill Lynch office where she lost her earlier investment. She was hired to fill their "women's quota," as she explained to *Publisher's Weekly*. She was informed that women weren't meant to work in this business and that she would be gone in six months.

When she started with Merrill Lynch, she was terrified of not making her sales quota. That is when she started writing affirmations every morning before heading to work. *I am young, powerful, and successful, producing at least $10,000 a month.* She commented, "I created what I wanted first on paper."

Now, Orman is a famed authority on finances and the author of the number-one New York Times bestseller, *The Nine Steps to Financial Freedom*. As she says, "My job is to be the financial truth crusader. Hope for the best. But plan for the worst."

Even when Orman surpassed her target goal, she carried her statement. "Like a lucky charm in words. I replaced the message of fear and my beliefs that I was inadequate with a message of endless possibility."

Cartoonist, Scott Adams, shares a similar method of setting a clear intention and following through to success. Adams started his career in a cubicle in corporate America. As a lowly technology worker he often occupied himself by doodling at his desk. Then he started writing over and over, *I will become a syndicated cartoonist.*

Adams had been rejected many times in his attempt to get his *Dilbert* comic strip published. Nevertheless, he persevered.

Finally the contract of his dreams to syndicate his column came through. Then he started writing, *I will become the greatest cartoonist.* You can be the judge of that as *Dilbert* is now syndicated in nearly 2000 newspapers worldwide. His *Dilbert Zone* website gets approximately 100,000 hits a day, and his first book, *The Dilbert Principle,* has sold more than 1.3 million copies. Plus, there are dozens of products using the Dilbert characters, everything from mouse pads, to coffee mugs, to tee-shirts, to calendars are on sale everywhere, and there is even a Dilbert television show.

Scott Adams believes that when you set an intention or write down a goal, "You'll observe things happening that will make that objective more likely to materialize." Adams advocates writing down your dreams and pursuing them step-by-step. It worked for him and it will work for you.

Years before everyone joined a gym and worked out diligently, exercise pioneer, Jack LaLanne, was passionate about his intention to teach people how to care for their bodies through weight lifting, aerobic exercise, and proper nutrition. He was an early leader of the movement for staying fit. His innovation in opening the first co-ed health club in 1936 was met with criticism. He was labeled radical, charlatan, crackpot and a nut, none of which curtailed his drive or determination. In fact, he followed his health club concept with an innovative fitness show on the growing medium of television.

LaLanne was never deterred by criticism because he approached his work with a single-minded focus. In an interview, he stated, "If you believe in something, if you practice what you preach you can't fail. I had a message. I wanted to help people. When you get something like that in your craw, you can't fail."

LaLanne had a clear intention, clarity of vision, and a determination to help.

It is a scientifically proven fact that the brain offers dramatic assistance once you set an intention. Researchers have proven the existence of a *reticular activating device*, which is part of the brain. It is located near the medulla oblongata at the base of the brain. Its function is to alert you when something is occurring that connects you to your goal or dream. You might note a heightened awareness or alertness when you meet certain people or attend an important event. Or, you may feel guided to a news article, a book, a television show, or a movie and discover that you have been the recipient of information or tools you need to pursue your goal.

If you go back in your memory, you will remember times when there were serendipitous happenings that moved you toward a desire for employment, or to buy a home, or to meet a friend. Some people compare this principle to following the prompts on a computer. Each one brings you closer to your goal. Each step is supplied at the exact right moment.

This principle also works in the political arena. As an illustration of setting an intention, American television correspondent Charles Osgood pointed to President John F. Kennedy's call in the early 1960's that America should put a man on the moon by the end of the decade. "There were lots of problems that would have to be solved—technical, political, and money problems— but Kennedy didn't try to solve them all in advance. All he did was set a definite timetable. He left it to others to work out how it was going to be done." And it was done. Neil Armstrong took his *giant leap for mankind* before the decade was over.

Set your intention. Make it clear and tangible. The subconscious mind has the ability to magnetize you to opportunities and opportunities to you when you set your mind with precision. The *reticular activating device* is ever at work, pointing the way. Like reaching the moon, be clear on what you want. Then get to it.

Writing down goals and dreams makes them clear and tangible.

Program Your Mind: Set Up Your Own Mental Software

Have you ever wondered why some people seem to live charmed lives and experience success in everything they do while others don't? There is a reason.

Successful people use the power of the subconscious mind to manifest the kind of lives they desire. The subconscious mind is a powerful creative ally, available for your use and direction. Not only does it hold memories and store information, it also contains a goal-seeking mechanism.

Many years ago, I read *Psycho Cybernetics* by Maxwell Maltz. In it, he said the most amazing thing that ultimately changed my own life. He stated that, "The subconscious mind does not know the difference between a real and an imagined experience." In other words, I could introduce an image or visualization into my mind with feeling, and the subconscious mind would consider it real and go about creating that exact experience.

This idea opened my mind to all kinds of possibilities. I immediately began to imagine and feel extra money pouring into my life. It was a simple visualization and accomplished with great excitement and joy. Within three weeks, my husband brought home a bonus check for $1000. This had never happened before. We were both excited and joyful.

At that point, it was an experiment. I didn't know what was going to happen. So, I decided to check out these results to make sure I had not inadvertently tapped into a coincidence. I did the whole visualization again. I decided that, if I was able to attract extra money into our lives a second time, it wasn't a coincidence, but rather, a result of my visualization. You can imagine my excitement when a few weeks later, my husband came home with another bonus check. This one for $2000. *Whoopee! Hallelujah! Yippee!* I was on to something.

These experiments began my study of the mind and everything that came with it. It became my passion. I had always wanted to understand how some things worked and why others didn't.

You, too, can discover the secret of manifesting the life you desire by applying the information in this chapter. It can change your life as it did mine. So, pay attention.

As you can imagine, I was at a new beginning when I discovered the power of the subconscious mind. I did not limit my creations to money for there were many other things I wanted to enjoy, like travel, flowers being delivered to me, a new job, an office, a car, a house, relationships, you name it. Over the years, creative visualization became my greatest tool in imagining life the way I wanted it. It will work for you, too.

The mind is a field of possibilities. Every possibility you can imagine exists. Many others you haven't thought about reside there as well. The idea is that you can choose the possibilities you want to experience. For example, if you believe you are unworthy and lacking talent, you probably register the possibility of being poor and struggling, What you believe weighs heavily into the way you direct your mind. If, conversely, you can imagine the possibility of great wealth and acclaim and let this idea become a dominant ideal in your mind, you will magnetize it to you.

Be clear, the mind is like a giant computer. It works according to the program or software you put into it. You get to choose what that program is. In fact, you are choosing it every day. Even when you buy into the idea that you have no say about something, you are following a program. It just happens to be the program of your parents, your friends, your teachers, or even your church. It could also be the suggestions given during the commercials on television. You know how it goes. "Do you have bumps on your skin? Chronic fatigue? Anxiety? Is your hair falling out? Do you sleep too much or not enough? If so, you have a terrible disease and you must take this drug."

Believe me, the television advertisers know all about mental suggestion. Many drugs and other products have been sold using images of happy, sad, depressed, thin, or laughing people. Babies and puppies work well, too. All of it suggests you can solve your problems if you buy their products.

The mind has no value system until you give it one. It does not consider anything a problem until you make it a problem. This could be such things as being overweight, being single or divorced, being a janitor, garbage collector, dropout, astronaut, millionaire, president of a company, etc. You are the one who makes these ideas important, relevant, and doable.

The mind, being a field of possibilities, accepts every possibility you dream up as valid. The more you embrace the dream, imagine it, feel it, and work toward it, the more readily it appears in your physical circumstances.

Another way to program your mind is through self-talk. You talk to yourself all day long. What are the things you say to yourself?

Recently, a female client was telling me her story. Every few sentences, she would reiterate that she did it wrong, or she

165

shouldn't have done this or that. "Someone is going to think badly of me. I'm so insecure. It is my insecurities that give me trouble." In other words, she was really being hard on herself. You might notice that her self-talk was very detrimental and non-affirming.

The problem is that we don't come into life with a manual. The whole process is a trial-and-error experience, from beginning to end. Plus, the parts of your psyche that are undeveloped will eventually become the focus points because we are here in earth school to learn to love ourselves.

If you are a person that doesn't give yourself credit and beats yourself up regularly for not knowing this or for doing that, you will magnetically attract people who will reinforce those habits. Why, you say? Because you have chosen to focus on the illusion that you are not good enough. Thus, that focus will be the study group you will be assigned to in earth school. Your assignment is to dispel the idea that you are anything but amazing, gorgeous, incredible, talented, and brilliant.

This beautiful lady who was so down on herself had the total package. She possessed all of these qualities, but was consumed with others' opinions of her. By the way, that is a sign of abuse. She was, in fact, a textbook case of an abused woman. She had been programmed to believe she was not good enough. Her internal wound created the illusion, "I am not good enough." A lot of pain surrounded that.

This is an example of mental programming. Through our work together, she will recognize the lie she has told herself. *Not good enough* was actually the interpretation she put on her inability to please her parents. That extended to her husband, and on and on from there

The truth is, she is not in the material world to please these people. That is their job. Her job is to please herself. All of these derogatory people drew her attention away from her inner beauty and light. They kept her distracted. When she began to re-program her mind with the truth of her amazing, creative, brilliant self, a different life came forth, along with new encouraging individuals.

Do you recognize yourself in this story? Most of us have been handed some negative mental programs, which we've converted into self-talk. What is most interesting about this fact is that we can use the same mechanism of self-talk to correct the mistake. Positive self-talk is one way to override past negative programming by erasing or replacing it with conscious, affirmative new directions. It is a practical way to live our lives, actively intending rather than passively accepting others' beliefs.

We are always talking to ourselves. We can even watch people chatting away in their heads. Sometimes they talk out loud.

When we use positive self-talk, we give ourselves new guidelines and set up our internal control centers with words and statements that are more helpful to the part of self we would like to improve. We design our self-talk statements around a new internal picture we would most like to exemplify.

To start, begin to observe your self-talk.

"I can't. I never should have. I'm tired and out of energy." These are self-demeaning statements that have to go.

"I should. I have to. I need to." These statements are not much better. These are still non-affirming declarations.

You cannot eliminate an idea without replacing it with something else. In other words, nature abhors a void and will fill it with something. Generally, it will fill it with what you are most used to:

your default self-talk. Therefore, you must be deliberate with what you intend to use to replace an old negative assertion.

Choosing a better you is the most powerful kind of self-talk. "I am a winner. I can do it. I am in control of my life. I am healthy, strong, and vivacious." These statements inspire, encourage, improve, and urge you forward.

As you use these proclamations, take a moment to envision this new, improved you. Negatively programmed beliefs keep you captive in a small consciousness. New expansive mental programs move you to a life of joy, expectation, and abundance.

Think about the areas of your life you would like to improve. Use self-talk and visualization to program your mind to create that advancement.

Start with some "I" statements. For example, "I am healthy, joy-filled, and vivacious." Say your statements with feeling.

Your turn:

- I am . . .

- I am . . .

- I am . . .

- I am . . .

Set aside five to ten minutes a day to visualize the results you seek and use positive affirmations to reinforce this picture.

Emotions Expand or Diminish You

Emotions are appreciated, as in the case of enthusiasm and joy, and they are decried, as with sadness and anger. But each emotion has a belief behind it and out of which it is born. For example, if you believe that everyone should like you and someone does not, your emotional reaction might be anger or resentment or hurt. If your belief is that when your favorite team wins, it is important to celebrate and feel happy, it might hold true for you that when they lose, feeling sad or melancholy is appropriate. Both reactions can be limiting because reacting to any external stimulus can be limiting.

Grief is caused by holding on to something past its time. We experience endings daily. It could be the death of a person, the loss of a job, the change of a situation, the dropping of an idea, the end of one day to be born into the next one. Everything is changing, evolving, and growing. Facing change and learning to let go will help you learn to flow and live in peace.

One widely held emotion is guilt. Many people are riddled with guilt over all kinds of things. Guilt about not being perfect. Guilt about seeing someone suffer and not doing something about it. In this case, the reaction of guilt doesn't take into account that there is value in suffering. Often, it is through suffering that people rise to their purpose and make changes.

For some, guilt arises from not giving enough attention, money, or accolades. Guilt is tied to many actions that come out of the word *should*. "I should be religious. I should visit my mother. I should care about the homeless. I should donate money. I should be nice." This is not to say that these actions aren't honorable, only that doing them out of guilt is wasteful and unrewarding.

The point is, emotions never stand alone. They are always connected to a deeper value, a belief system that you have put in place. To become fully empowered so that you can do the impossible, you are required to examine your belief systems. How do you know what they are? Pay attention to your reactions. Where and when do you feel emotional? Discovering your trigger points, positive and negative, will help you identify beliefs and ideals that lie beneath the surface of your mind.

There are many people who think that life should be *fair*. When they encounter unfairness in any form, they get upset. The interesting thing about the subject of unfairness is that it looks different to each person. For example, someone may hold the idea that living without sufficient food is unfair. When they recognize that the person doing without food refuses to work and wants, instead, to be taken care of, to live off public largess, they may find that unfairness is not the issue.

There are many ways to view a situation. Your perception is only one.

Regardless, we have the ability to recognize our emotional reactions and trace them back to their origin. This can be done with the mental discipline to observe and become quietly objective. With practice, you will be able to let go of emotions that take up space in your mind and serve no useful purpose.

There is such a thing as emotional genius. Karla McLaren, respected healer and author of *Emotional Genius: Discovering the Deepest Language of the Soul,* tells us, "Emotions are celebrated and repressed, analyzed and medicated, adored and ignored, but rarely, are they honored. Yet, when understood, emotions reveal practical tools that we can use to stop struggling in relationships, family, career, and personal growth."

For example, anger can reveal key insights necessary to change a self-defeating behavior that can interfere with success. Fear holds memories that may be helpful in effectively resolving crisis. Depression, by its very name, indicates repressed desires. It has also been said that *body fat* represents unfulfilled dreams. This is, yet, another sign of repression.

By getting in touch with emotions, rather than running from them, we might embrace our most passionate inner desires, go on to fulfill them, and return, once again, to a natural state of joy. What is it you really want to do or experience that you are not allowing? Observe your emotional reactions around people, events, and activities, and you will receive valuable cues regarding your *real* desires. What activity brings you the most joy? Passion? Satisfaction?

Recently, I spent time with Roland, who often used the word *but.* "I want to do that, but I may not have the time. I understand what you are saying, but it doesn't work for me."

Roland was protecting himself from receiving new ideas. It was such a strong habit that he didn't know he was doing it. As we spoke, he revealed that he grew up protecting himself from his father's threatening demeanor and his mother's interrogation. Even though they were long gone, Roland was still living with his parents. There was no longer anything from which Roland needed protection. What he was really accomplishing was keeping himself imprisoned in his small space and locking the world out. This resulted in his loneliness. Can you see that, for Roland to create community, he had to open himself to others' energy, ideas, and ways of being. He didn't have to *become* them, just be *open* to them. Also, he had to let himself feel safe.

Emotions contain a vast reservoir of information linking us to our Higher Intelligence. By connecting with our emotional selves, we can regain direction, key into our greatest talents, reenergize our bodies, and live an inspired life. Conversely, by thwarting ourselves emotionally, we lose connection with our passions and inspirations. According to Karla McLaren, how well we use our emotional resources determines our emotional genius.

Answer these questions:

What am I feeling right now?

What issue evokes the greatest amount of emotion in your life? Unfairness? Lack of control? Disrespect? Dishonesty? Something else?

How do you block yourself from feeling?

In what area of your life do you need to offer forgiveness?

Turn Fear into Love

There are ultimately only two emotions: love and fear. The energy of love is light, airy, pleasant. Whereas, the energy of fear is heavy, dark, restrictive, and closed. Love energy can be felt as peace, joy, happiness, compassion, abundance, enthusiasm, gratitude, and motivation. Fear is experienced as anger, resentment, guilt, annoyance, worry, resistance, anxiety.

You can tell if you are experiencing love or fear by paying attention to your body. Is it tight, tense, rigid, or flowing, at ease, relaxed. Tightness is fear. Flow and ease reflect love. You can monitor your emotions and note whether love or fear dominates your mind.

A fear-based person focuses on what is missing, what is wrong, what he doesn't have. This promotes a sense of restriction, smallness, and closed-mindedness. Fearful people lack the vision and courage to try something new or explore unseen territories. Instead, they stick with the known, the usual patterns, routines, and relationships. They repeat themselves, hoping they won't make mistakes or look foolish. Concern over failing is a major consideration because they are object-oriented, which means they are focused on the external world and affected by others' opinions. They tend to set their course accordingly.

Because the opposite of fear is love, there is always opportunity to switch your focus from fear to love. A natural expansion comes with making decisions from a consciousness of love. Anything is possible. You can accomplish anything when you live from a vast, expanded point of view. This is definitely preferable to living in a restrictive, joyless, fear-based consciousness.

The focus, when learning to live from love, is self-orientation. This means that the individual is conscious and continually determining right action, while maintaining integrity, personal values, and advancing along a positive course. Love nurtures and encourages flow, ease, and peace, which is felt in the body as vibrancy and health.

India's leader, Mahatma Gandhi, was an example of love-based thinking. He made decisions based on principles of what was the highest good for his nation. He sought freedom from prejudicial treatment and unfair practices. Gandhi led a peaceful revolution that altered the political landscape in India. He did so without violence. He was an incredibly creative, forward-thinking individual. His actions ultimately paved the way for Dr. Martin Luther King, Jr. to do the same in the United States. King's philosophy was love-based, encouraging expansion and freedom for all while causing harm to no one.

All the people in your life express these two energies. You can tell if you are in the right relationships by the energy you feel. If your association is not enriching and elevating, it is fear-based. On the contrary, a healthy, love-based relationship enriches and lifts both parties.

The same is true for jobs, careers, and professions. If you are uncomfortable and restrained, your approach to work is fear-based. Contrarily, when you feel light, happy, and free in relationship or career, you are experiencing love.

We all want love, acceptance, and empathy in our lives, but are we making the right choices to experience these things? To have love, we must give love. What we give away comes back to us by the law of energy. As we extend light-hearted feelings of helpfulness, support, and acceptance, we naturally move toward those who offer the same.

There is a saying: "By your actions, you will be known." It means simply that the energy you express through your actions speaks volumes about you. Your words are meaningless next to your actions. How are you expressing your energy? Is it loving and supportive or angry and blaming? Are you congruent in your beliefs, values, and actions? Meaning, do your actions and words match each other, or are you saying one thing and doing another?

Recently, a client called and stated that she felt out of control with anxiety and fear. She said she needed immediate help to gain control over her mind, which was dominated with fear.

I gave her a technique. "Move your mind to gratitude. The mind cannot be fearful and grateful at the same time."

The mind can only focus on one thing at a time. Even people who feel they are multitaskers, focus on one thing at a time and move every few seconds. At any one moment, they are focusing on one idea, concept, or task. Because they switch focus often, they can end up feeling incomplete or unfulfilled with a particular task. In addition, they may not remember what they accomplished or where they left off.

The key is to decide what you want to feel and focus on that. Do not shift your focus until you have manifested your desire. If you want to live a life of peace and love, keep your attention there.

When you choose to look to the positive, to the possibilities for goodness, to expectations of things working out, you are operating from love. When you choose to experience love, you are open to a full array of positive possibilities.

When you fill your mind with fear and *what-ifs*, your mind closes to the idea that things can work out. What-ifs steer you to the world of form, or what appears to be an external reality. Externals are constantly changing. So, what appeared to be real one moment, will change in the next. For example, a tree goes through phenomenal changes with each season. All of nature and life is in continuous motion, changing with every breeze and every drop of water. The world of form is constantly evolving as well.

Here is the simple exercise I told my client and you can use to shift your mind to openness, expansiveness, and positivity. Move into gratitude. What can you be grateful for right now? Referring to your present situation, what might you feel grateful about? How might you see it from a higher perspective?

You can be thankful for sunshine, trees, your home (no matter how humble), comfort, food, friendship, kindness, and opportunities of every type. You can be joyful for your breath, for your health, for being able to walk, communicate, smile, and reach out to help others. Once you stop and check, you will realize you have much to be appreciative for, and that begins the process of converting your thinking to the expansive energy of success, love, kindness, goodness, abundance, health, and joy. It sets you up to accomplish the most outrageous things, because there are no limits when you decide to live in love.

Trust the dreams, for in them
is hidden the gate to eternity.

—Khalil Gibran, Persian Poet

Just become quiet, still, and solitary,
and the world will offer itself to you to be unmasked;
it has no choice. It will roll in ecstasy at your feet.

—Franz Kafka, Writer and Novelist

It is not a magic feather; it is you who can fly.

—Dumbo, The Flying Elephant

■

Chapter Twelve

Conclusion

We have been taught through our earthly experiences that we are to accumulate wealth and draw acclaim and honor. That is the picture of success we've been given. Yet, when you embrace your highest truth, purpose, and ideals, you discover a source of wisdom and light that goes beyond human description. That is when you recognize your own creativity, brilliance, and beauty. It is true for everyone. You are a blessing to all people and present to make a difference, to enrich the world.

Mother Theresa, Mahatma Gandhi, Martin Luther King Jr., Jesus, and many great leaders were not materially wealthy, yet they were successful. They followed an inner guidance system that superseded finite wealth. They were outrageous in what they shared and taught. They left their mark on mankind forever in all countries and for all generations. This is not to indicate that money, gold, fine houses, or cars are bad, only that they are but one element of wealth. Don't overlook the others.

Through these chapters, you have read stories of outrageous people doing what seemed like the impossible. Each left their unique mark, like Harriet Tubman in denouncing slavery and working for equality, like Wil Smith in caring for his infant daughter despite the challenge of youth and inexperience, like Layne Walker becoming a writer, publisher, and artist notwithstanding being a high-school dropout, like Thomas Edison inventing in spite of the handicap of deafness and being told he was stupid, and like Kyle Maynard who, regardless of considerable physical disabilities, showed the world that anything can be accomplished when one sets one's mind and heart to it.

Each of these individuals connected to a source of energy and vision that went beyond formal education, societal training, and dogma. They connected with a soul desire that drove them to accomplish impossible feats and stood to inspire all of us. In that way, they changed the world.

All accomplishments, big and small, bear the signature of heroism. Each person has within himself genius, creativity, heroism, and the inherent ability to do what appears to be impossible. We are heroes in that we are here to heal past wounds, to courageously face our supposed limitations, to deal with our adversarial beliefs, and to achieve the impossible.

What is the drive behind your actions?

A child that has been put down and abused can grow up to prove that the opposite can be true, that he is good enough, that he is talented, creative, and loveable. He can become a leader, scholar, inventor, writer, or anything else and receive great acclaim. Or, he can go the other way into poverty and live the example and prophecy of his abuser.

I offer you the message of this book with a wish that you make a connection to your own heroic self and offer it to the world in the spirit of healing. This will be accomplished through the inspiration you offer. As you perceive your situation with new eyes, you will see the possibilities to break through to a higher purpose.

What great lesson are you here to learn? Unconditional love? Perseverance? Strength of purpose? Unleashing your creativity and inventiveness? Taking action despite negative opinions?

What wound are you here to heal? What limitation have you taken to heart and accepted as truth?

Now is your time to observe with new eyes.

Your inner urge will guide you to your outrageous life. It makes you special. Listen to it. Let it be your guide. It will lead you to your genius, whether that be running a great race, preparing a nutritious meal, or healing the sick and wounded. You may have to throw off the mantle of cultural beliefs and limitations to really hear this internal voice, but as outlined in this book, you may have gained many indications as to what that urge is. Clues, symbols, and indications will keep coming. Spirit is persistent.

I leave you with these truths:

- We are all one in Spirit.
- What you do for others, you also do for yourself.
- You are being guided to a higher purpose.
- Listen!

I send my blessings to you as you embrace your amazing path of inspired creativity and guidance. May you truly live your impossible dreams and be outrageously successful. May you recognize that everything is possible because YOU are bringing your amazing self to the task.

About the Author

Jean Walters is a Saint Louis based teacher of self-empowerment principles for over thirty years. She has studied metaphysics extensively and applies universal principles to every area of her life.

Walters has written weekly and monthly columns for major Saint Louis newspapers and publications and been published as a free-lance author all over the United States. *Besides Be Outrageous: Do the Impossible—Others have; you can too!*, she has written: *Set Yourself Free: Live the life YOU were meant to Live,* and *Dreams and the Symbology of Life.*

Her radio show, Positive Moments, was syndicated on 110 stations across the nation and she has been a featured guest on many radio and television shows, even being referred to as The Dream Lady on several stations. This is a result of her ability to interpret listeners' dreams over the air.

Walters has designed and presented classes and workshops in empowerment, meditation, building communication skills, universal laws, dream interpretation, strengthening intuition, and creating spiritual connection for many organizations, colleges, universities, spiritual groups, and businesses around the Midwest. She continues to offer her services to empower others.

From her office in Saint Louis, Missouri, she works with people around the world as a Transformational Coach and Akashic Record reader (psychic). She has performed over 35,000 readings with the emphasis on providing insight regarding personal growth, life purpose, strengthening relationships, and moving through obstacles. She has been presented with the "Best Psychic in Saint Louis" award for the last eight years.

Jean's mission is to lead people to the Light—to encourage, guide and assist others to live freely and express from their Highest Selves.

You can reach her through her website: www.spiritualtransformation.com

Or jean@spiritualtransformation.com